Sustainable Public Procurement: A Global Review
Final Report

December 2013

Acknowledgements

UNEP gratefully acknowledges the time and effort spent by those involved in producing and commenting on this "Sustainable Public Procurement: A Global Review".

The report was authored by: Dr. Anastasia O'Rourke (Big Room Inc.), Dr. Charlotte Leire (Lund University, Sweden) and Trevor Bowden (Big Room Inc.) under the supervision of Farid Yaker (UNEP) and Carlos Andrés Enmanuel (UNEP).

We would like to extend our appreciation and thanks to the following individuals for their support in the development, interviews and review of the report: Fanny Demassieux — United Nations Environment Programme (UNEP); Zuzana Baranovi ová — Slovenská agentúra životného prostredia; Ian Barham — United Kingdom Department for Environment, Food and Rural Affairs (UK DEFRA), Alenka Burja — Ministry of Agriculture and Environment of Slovenia; Sylvain Chevassus — Ministère de l'écologie, du développement durable et de l'énergie de France; Dr. Carl Dalhammar — IIIEE Lund University; Mats Ekenger — Nordic Council of Ministers; Dr. Handito Joewono — Green Purchasing Network Indonesia (GPNI); Akira Kataoka — International Green Purchasing Network (IGPN); Robert Kaukewitsch — European Commission; Alison Kinn Bennett — United States Environmental Protection Agency (US EPA); Augustine Koh — Green Purchasing Network Malaysian (GPNM); Sanjay Kumar — Indian Railways; Jacob Malthouse — Big Room Inc.; Barbara Morton — Sustainable Procurement Ltd.; Peter Nohrstedt — Swedish Environmental Management Council (SEMCo); Jason Pearson — Sustainable Purchasing Council; Miguel Porrua — Organization of American States (OAS); Pablo A. Prüssing Fuchslocher — Dirección ChileCompra; Niels Ramm — United Nations Office for Project Services (UNOPS); Abby Semple — Procurement Analysis; Yalmaz Siddiqui — Office Depot; Maria Sundesten — The Nordic Swan; Norma Tregurtha — ISEAL Alliance.

UNEP would also like to convey its gratitude to the respondents of the pilot survey, which was instrumental for the development of the report: Jerry Sebastian Ackotia — Public Procurement Authority of Ghana; Aure Adell — Ecoinstitut; Thad Carlson — Best Buy Co., Inc.; Scot Case — UL Environment; Helena Fonseca — Organization of American States (OAS); Bettina Schaefer — Ecoinstitut; Shirley Soto Montero — Ministerio de Ambiente, Energía y Mares de Costa Rica; Sacheedanand Tahalooa — Ministry of Finance of Mauritius.

Table of Contents

Abbreviations and Acronyms

EFTA	European Free Trade Association
EC	European Commission
EU	European Union
EO	Executive Order
EPEAT	Electronic Product Environmental Assessment Tool
EPP	Environmentally Preferable Procurement
GA	General Assembly
GDP	Gross Domestic Product
GPP	Green Public Procurement
ICLEI	International Council on Local Environmental Initiatives
ILO	International Labour Organization
IISD	International Institute for Sustainable Development
IGO	Intergovernmental Organization
IGPN	International Green Purchasing Network
IPCC	Intergovernmental Panel on Climate Change
ISO	International Organization for Standardization
ICT	Information Communication Technology
IT	Information Technology
ITC	International Training Centre
JRC-IPTS	Joint Research Centre's Institute for Prospective Technological Studies (European Union)
KPI	Key Performance Indicators
LCC	Life Cycle Costing
MDB	Multilateral Development Bank
MDGs	Millennium Development Goals
MERCOSUR	El Mercado Común del Sur
MTF	Marrakech Task Force
NAFTA	North American Free Trade Agreement
NAGPI	North American Green Purchasing Initiative
NAP	National Action Plan
NASPO	National Association of State and Local Procurement Officers
OAS	Organization of American States
OECD	Organisation for Economic Co-operation and Development
RPN	Responsible Purchasing Network
SME	Small and Medium-sized Enterprises
SP	Sustainable Procurement
SCP	Sustainable Consumption and Production
SPP	Sustainable Public Procurement
SPP/GPP	Sustainable Public Procurement/Green Public Procurement
SPPI	Sustainable Public Procurement Initiative
SUN	Sustainable United Nations
UK	United Kingdom
UN	United Nations
UNCITRAL	United Nations Commission on International Trade Law
UNFCCC	United Nations Framework Convention on Climate Change
UNEP	United Nations Environment Programme
UNOPS	United Nations Office for Project Services
UNPD	United Nations Procurement Division
USA	United States of America
USEPA	United States Environmental Protection Agency
WLC	Whole-life costing
WTO	World Trade Organization

1. Introduction

With governments responsible for significant portions of national spending — up to 30 per cent of gross domestic product (GDP) in some cases[1] — the promise of "greening" spending can enable policy makers to "lead by example" when it comes to sustainable development. By doing so, they can lead vast supply chains towards implementing more sustainable practices, achieving environmental, social, and economic policy objectives.

Around the world, interest in Sustainable Public Procurement (SPP) / Green Public Procurement (GPP) is growing. In an interview conducted for this report, Augustine Koh of the Malaysian Green Purchasing Network said, "From green pillows to green food, buyers and sellers are all talking green now".

Sustainable Public Procurement is at the core of international cooperation processes on Sustainable Consumption and Production (SCP). SPP features indeed as one of the five initial programmes of the 10-Year Framework of Programmes on SCP (10YFP), a global framework of action adopted by the Rio+20 Conference to accelerate the shift towards SCP in both developed and developing countries.

SPP/GPP is now at a critical juncture. While a great deal of work has been done in the last five years and at least 43 countries now have public institutions that have adopted an SPP/GPP policy or policy measures, difficult economic conditions may counter this trend. Barriers such as the persistent idea that these products are more expensive may also hinder further progress. Moreover, the multitude of different systems, criteria and approaches to SPP/GPP risks confusing suppliers and purchasers, further slowing progress. It is therefore timely that a review of the current state of SPP/GPP is undertaken worldwide and critical to better understanding how SPP/GPP is contributing to the creation of a robust "Green Economy".[2]

This report contains the findings of an investigation into the national government SPP/GPP policies and practices around the world. The policies, programmes, drivers, barriers, needs and opportunities in SPP/GPP are examined, based on an analysis of recent literature and online resources, and interviews with 20 leading experts on SPP/GPP. Six case studies that delve deeper into particular countries' recent experiences with SPP/GPP accompany the report. The result is a global view that considers the challenges and opportunities for SPP/GPP in different governmental, regulatory and socio-economic contexts, and highlights the evolution of SPP/GPP in recent years.

The report has two objectives — to provide a qualitative overview of the drivers, challenges and trends in SPP/GPP, and to articulate a framework for subsequent quantitative data gathering.

The research was commissioned by UNEP, having identified the need for up-to-date and reliable information on activities and organizations involved in SPP/GPP. UNEP and various partners announced at Rio+20 the launch of a Sustainable Public Procurement Initiative (SPPI)[3] to fast track a global transition to a green economy by harnessing the market-shifting power of government and local authority spending. The SPPI builds on the work of the Swiss-led Marrakech Task Force on Sustainable Public Procurement that ended its mandate in May 2011.[4]

Supported by over 45 governments and institutions, the international SPPI aims to scale-up the level of public spending flowing into goods and services that maximize environmental and social benefits. The goal is to promote worldwide implementation of SPP/GPP through increased cooperation between key stakeholders and a better understanding of its benefits and impacts. The objectives are to bring together representatives from governments, local authorities, business sector and civil society interested in promoting the supply and demand of sustainable products through SPP/GPP and then collectively:

- Build the case for SPP/GPP, increasing knowledge on SPP/GPP and its effectiveness as a tool to promote greener economies and sustainable development; and

- Support the implementation of SPP/GPP through collaboration and better access to capacity building tools.

---

1   OECD, 2002b.

2   UNEP, 2011 identified SPP as a key "enabling condition" towards the transition towards a Green Economy.

3   UNEP DTIE, SPP Programme See: http://www.unep.fr/scp/procurement/

4   The Marrakech Task Forces (MTF) are voluntary initiatives, led by governments, which - in co-operation with various other partners from the North and the South - commit themselves to carrying out a set of activities, at the national or regional level, that promote a shift to consumption and production patterns towards greater sustainability. The Marrakech Process responds to the call of the Johannesburg Plan of Implementation (2002) to develop a 10-Year Framework of Programmes on Sustainable Consumption and Production.

The 10-Year Framework of Programmes on Sustainable Consumption and Production

At the United Nations Conference on Sustainable Development (Rio+20), Heads of State strengthened their commitment to accelerate the shift towards SCP patterns with the adoption of the 10-Year Framework of Programmes on Sustainable Consumption and Production Patterns (10YFP), in paragraph 226 of the Outcome Document "The Future We Want". The 10YFP is a concrete and operational outcome of Rio+20. It responds to the 2002 Johannesburg Plan of Implementation, and builds on the eight years work and experience of the Marrakech Process — a bottom-up multi-stakeholder process, launched in 2003 with strong and active involvement from all regions.

Main objectives

As a global framework of action to enhance international cooperation to accelerate the shift towards SCP in both developed and developing countries, the main objectives of the 10YFP include:

- Support regional and national policies and initiatives to accelerate the shift towards SCP, contributing to resource efficiency and decoupling economic growth from environmental degradation and resource use, while creating new job/market opportunities and contributing to poverty eradication and social development.

- Mainstream SCP into sustainable development policies, programmes and strategies, as appropriate, including into poverty reduction strategies.

- Provide financial and technical assistance and capacity building to developing countries, supporting the implementation of SCP activities at the regional and national levels.

- Enable all stakeholders (government, private sector, civil society, researchers, UN agencies, financial institutions, and other major groups) to share information and knowledge on SCP tools, initiatives and best practices, raising awareness and enhancing cooperation and development of new partnerships — including public-private partnerships.

Programmes

Programmes are at the core of the framework. They will:

- contribute to further promoting and implementing SCP;
- bring together existing initiatives and partnerships working in similar areas;
- build synergies and cooperation between stakeholders to leverage resources towards mutual objectives, and
- minimize duplication of ongoing efforts.

The programmes will contribute to meeting the goals and principles of the 10YFP responding to national and regional needs, priorities and circumstances. They will encourage the involvement of governments, business, civil society and all relevant stakeholders. The programmes will use a mix of policy instruments and set clear objective, activities and indicators of success.

The 10YFP adopted text includes an indicative and open list of programmes, which builds primarily on the experience gained through the Marrakech Process, including its Task Forces and regional SCP roundtables and strategies. The five initial programmes are:

i. consumer information;

ii. sustainable lifestyles and education;

iii. sustainable public procurement (SPP);

iv. sustainable buildings and construction; and

v. sustainable tourism, including ecotourism.

There is the possibility to build additional programmes, should countries demand them.

2. Scope and Methodology

2.1 Research Scope

The main focus for the research was national governments' work on SPP/GPP in the past five years. The scope of this study is global, however not all national SPP/GPP initiatives and programmes were surveyed. Existing data, examples and best practices that might be of interest and use to other SPP/GPP policymakers and practitioners were researched. These findings were further validated with a survey of over 250 SPP/GPP practitioners worldwide.

A 2007 Report on the State of Play in Sustainable Public Procurement by IISD[5] served as a starting point for this research. The last five years of activities are the focus of this report, and in addressing future plans, the scope is the coming five-year period. In assessing SPP/GPP, a long-term view is needed. Shifting an embedded and institutionalized procedure such as public procurement is a significant undertaking that also needs to happen in tandem with the sustainable transformation of markets and industry.

Workstreams	Subgroups	Lead Organization
Working Group 1: Proposing a vision and purchasing principles	Subgroup 1A: Developing Principles for SPP	TBD
	Subgroup 1B: Proposing a vision for Sustainable Procurement	VARRIO 40
Working Group 2: Monitoring SPP/GPP implementation and assessing impacts	Subgroup 2A: Monitoring SPP Implementation	Ecoinstitut Barcelona
	Subgroup 2B: Measuring and Communicating the Benefits Created by SPP	DEKRA
	Subgroup 2C: Promoting Best Practices	OECD, UNEP
Working Group 3: Addressing barriers to SPP implementation and proposing/disseminating innovative solutions	Subgroup 3A: Integrating Product Service Systems in Sustainable Public Procurement	USEPA, UNEP
	Subgroup 3B: Addressing Legal Barriers	Judge Marc Steiner/UNEP
Working Group 4: Promoting collaboration with the private sector	Subgroup 4A: Greening Supply Chains	SEMCo
	Subgroup 4B: Supporting SPP implementation through the use of Eco-labelling and Sustainability Standards	UNEP, ISEAL
Working Group 5: Cooperating for SPP implementation	Subgroup 5A: Improving the collaboration between central and local governments	TBD
	Subgroup 5B: Collaboration with IGOs and MDBs	TBD
Core Activities		
Management of the Multistakeholder Advisory Committee		Coordinating Office
Coordination of SPP Implementation Group		Coordinating Office
Biennial SPP Report		Coordinating Office
SPPI Forum		Coordinating Office
Communication activities (Website, Global SCP Clearinghouse, Social Networks)		Coordinating Office

Figure 1: An Overview of the Sustainable Public Procurement Initiative (SPPI)[6]

---

5   Oshani et al., 2007
6   http://www.sppinitiative.org

2.2 Research Methods and Data

The research undertaken for this report was reliant on existing literature and participation from survey respondents and experts, and was not based on a country-by-country monitoring and reporting exercise.

Findings are based on the following research and data sources:

Literature Review: A comprehensive literature review of reports on regional and national level SPP/GPP, including academic and other studies was conducted. In all, some 174 reports and articles were identified, mainly covering the last five years of SPP/GPP activity.

Online Resources: Data, reports, and other information published by UNEP, ICLEI Local Governments for Sustainability, the European Commission (EC), the International Green Purchasing Network (IGPN), the Responsible Purchasing Network (RPN) and other initiatives that promote and expand SPP/GPP activities were gathered. In addition, online material posted by national governments on their SPP/GPP programmes and activities was reviewed where relevant.

Interviews: Twenty experts and practitioners on SPP/GPP from 12 countries were interviewed as part of the research (see Appendix 3 for the list of interviewees). The interview subjects were selected to reflect different stakeholder and regional perspectives. Questions were sent in advance and interviews were conducted by telephone over one-hour in a semi-structured format. Notes were taken but the interviews were not recorded.

Country Case Studies: Appendix 1 of the report presents six short case studies on SPP/GPP on Chile, India, the European Union, Japan, Slovenia and the United States of America (USA). These were selected to show a range of activities from leading SPP regions (as nominated by interviewees and UNEP experts) and to highlight new and interesting activities on SPP/GPP. Experts in each of these countries/regions fact-checked the cases and provided feedback on them.

Survey: An international survey was undertaken with government procurement officers, experts and other stakeholders to SPP/GPP participating. The survey was conducted between September 5 and October 5, 2012 and drew 273 respondents, as described below.

2.3 Survey Methodology and Sample

The survey on current SPP/GPP practice worldwide was conducted using a customised web-based survey tool accessed by an email invitation. The survey questions were informed by an interim version of the report that was based on the findings of the literature review, desktop research, interviews and case studies. A draft set of questions was reviewed by a panel of 13 experts, then further tested and refined following a "pilot" test by individuals from nine organizations representing different stakeholder views. A list of who reviewed and piloted the survey can be found in Appendix 3 and survey questions are available upon request.

The survey was intended to gather both quantitative data on SPP/GPP as well as more qualitative and opinion-based perspectives. Most questions were multiple-choice and the order of options appeared to respondents was randomised to reduce the bias towards selecting the first few in the list provided. Beyond the set answer options, respondents were also able to provide comments to provide a different option or further explain their response.

The survey was designed to split respondents based on their stakeholder group. National government agency representatives answered survey 1 questions; and all other stakeholders answered survey 2 questions. Seventeen questions were common to both surveys. Results in the report indicate which group the survey data presented refers to. Some of the questions were conditional on prior questions and some respondents opted to skip some of the questions.

A total of 2,224 people were invited to participate in the survey via email and a letter of invitation. Recipients were gathered from a database of national government and other stakeholders working on SPP/GPP maintained by UNEP's Sustainable Consumption and Production Branch, within the Division of Technology, Industry, and Economics. In addition, partner organization IGPN sent the survey invitation to its network of national green procurement programs.

The total number of respondents to the survey was 273, representing a 12 per cent response rate. Of those, 40 per cent (110 respondents) answered the first portion of the survey, and 60 per cent (163 respondents) answered the second portion of the survey.

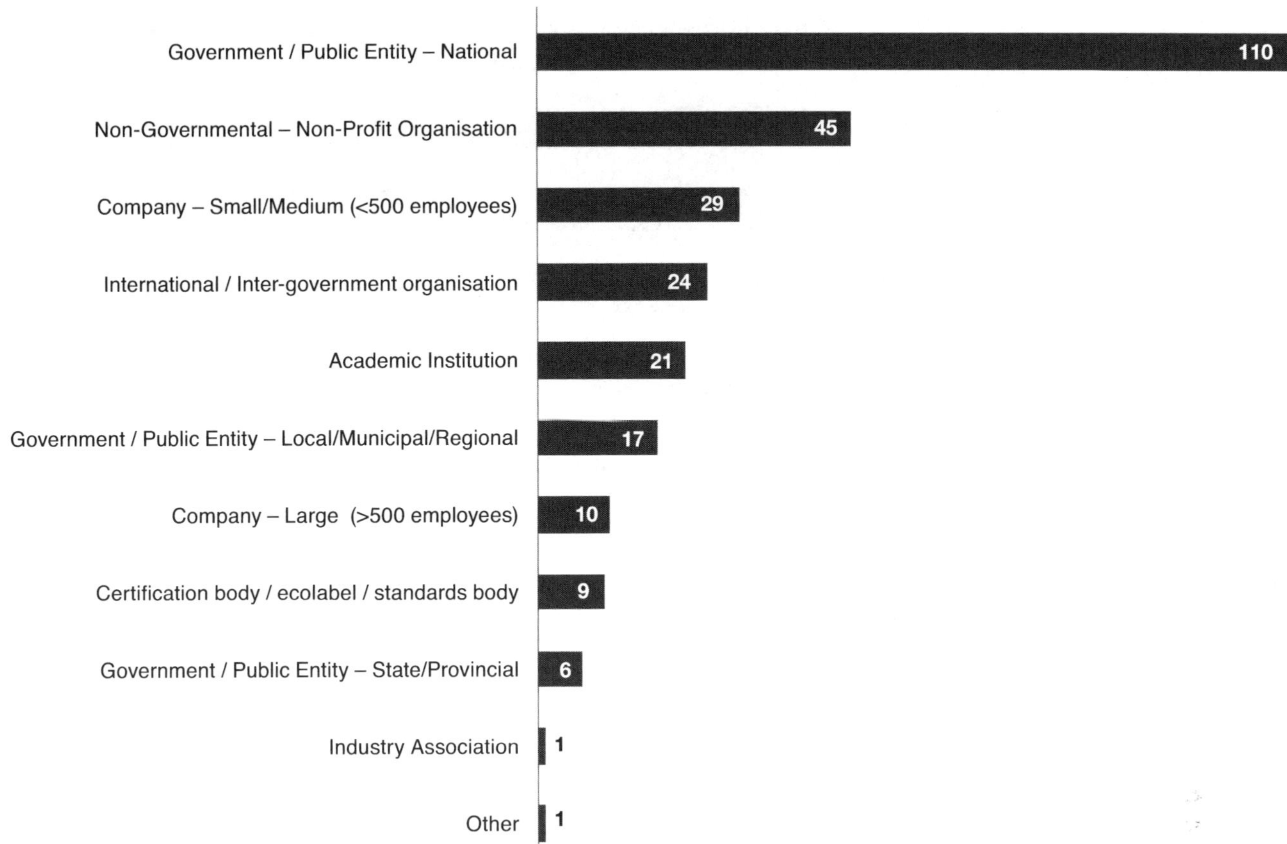

Figure 2: Types of organizations that responded to the survey

In some cases, more than one national government representative from the same country provided a response, oftentimes they were working in different departments or agencies. For those questions in the survey aimed at gathering a country-by country view of SPP/GPP (some 16 questions), each country was only counted once. If there was a discrepancy between how the different national government respondents from the same country answered, the answers provided were fact-checked against the given policy document/action plan or regulation and/or further confirmed with the respondents via email.

Figure 2 shows the other types of stakeholders (beyond national governments) who participated in the survey. After national governments, the second largest category of respondents was non-governmental organizations at 16, then companies (small/medium at 10 per cent and large companies at 4 per cent). The proportion of respondents from large companies was relatively small, especially compared to their influence on sustainable consumption and production practices.

Figure 3 illustrates the different ways that the non-national government respondents are engaged in SPP/GPP, from providing information, advocating for SPP/GPP, consulting, training and conducting research on SPP/GPP. Other activities mentioned included "facilitating market access to fair trade products", "participating in international cooperation" and "developing SPP/GPP guidelines for my non-governmental organization".

The category of regional and local governments attracted some respondents. While significant work is being undertaken on SPP/GPP at the regional/state and local level of government around the world[7], this report and survey was focused on the activities of national governments.

Figure 4 shows the breakdown of survey respondents by world region.[8]

Participants in the survey came from many different regions. Some 53 per cent of respondents came from outside North America and Europe (where many other studies on SPP/GPP tend to focus). The largest regional proportion of respondents came from Europe, followed by Africa, North America, then Asia. Oceania was not well represented in the

---

7   See ICLEI, ProcuraPlus, http://www.procuraplus.org

8   Countries were coded by region using the United Nations Statistical Division's macro geographical (continental) regions. UN Statistics Division, 2012.

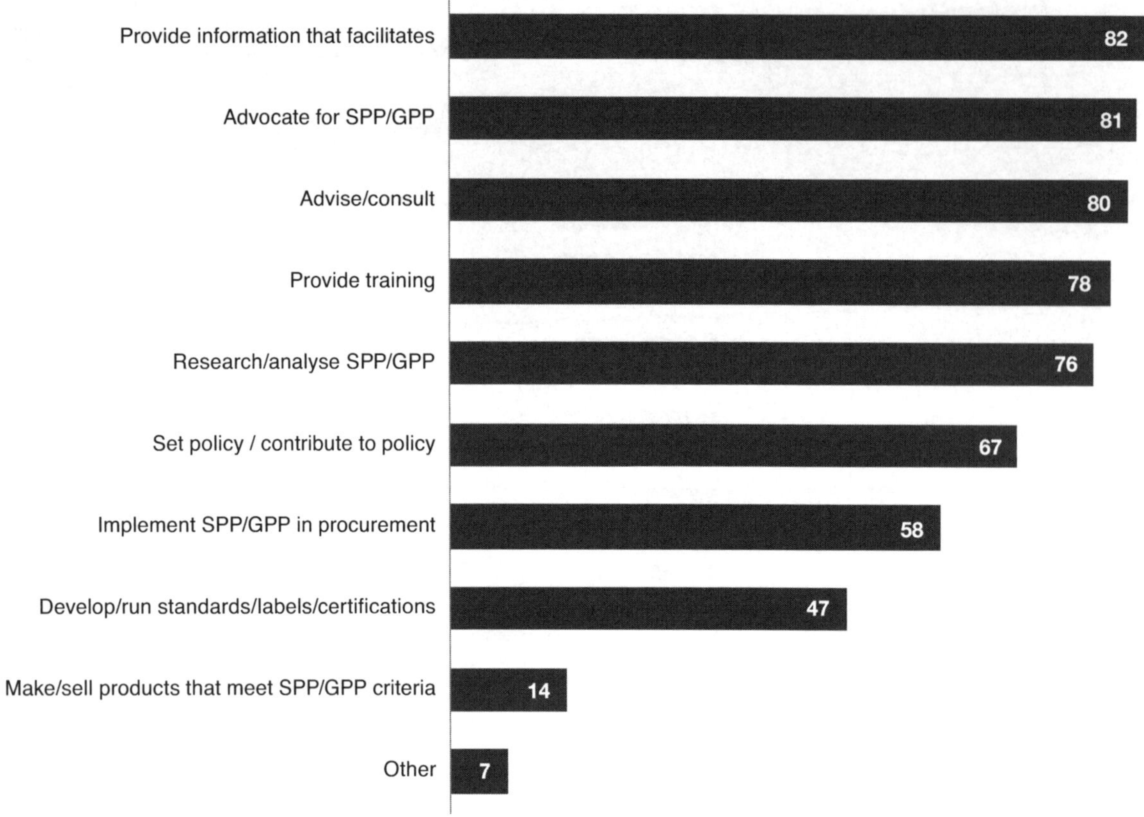

Figure 3: Non-national government survey respondents' involvement in SPP/GPP

survey, which is not indicative of the level of interest and activity on SPP/GPP in the region.[9] The largest single group or respondents was from the USA, with some 44 respondents. The second largest group of respondents was Tunisia, with ten respondents, then Malaysia, Spain and Switzerland, all with nine respondents each.

Respondents from 92 different countries took the survey, and respondents working for national government agencies came from 62 countries. There were a higher proportion of national government respondents coming from Africa and Latin/Central America than for the survey population as a whole. National government respondents were split between those working in procurement agencies (33 per cent), environmental agencies (30 per cent) and finance ministries (9 per cent). A large proportion (28 per cent) of respondents selected "other", including: International Development/Aid; Energy; Training/Capacity Building; Construction; Agriculture and others. This shows that there is participation in SPP/GPP beyond just procurement and sustainability agencies, and that many different organizations are currently interested and involved in SPP/GPP.

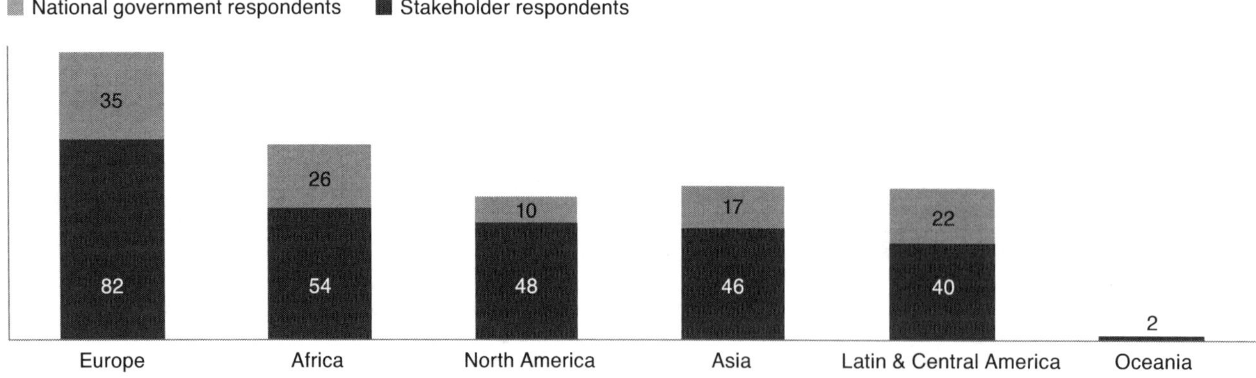

Figure 4: The number of Survey Respondents by Region and Type

---

9   See for example the work being undertaken in New Zealand: NZ Business Council for Sustainable Development, 2009.

2.4 Study Limitations

The majority of interviews were conducted in English. The literature reviewed was primarily in English, Portuguese, Spanish, and Swedish, reflecting the language constraints of the research team. Where possible, literature and online material was also gathered in other languages and was translated using online tools. The survey was conducted in English, although some comments were received in other languages, which were then translated by UNEP staff. By necessity, the research was limited to those countries and initiatives that are actively communicating about their work to external audiences and in formats that are accessible to international audiences.

Given the limitations of this research, there is likely to be much more activity on SPP/GPP by national governments than is covered in the report. Due to the size of national spending and dynamism of SPP/GPP in particular it is not feasible to report on all activities worldwide. Therefore, this report only provides a snapshot of SPP/GPP efforts, focusing on trends, obstacles and emerging solutions internationally.

One of aims of the research was to lay the foundation for the collection and dissemination of SPP/GPP activities worldwide and begin a dialogue on how that best be achieved with relevant stakeholders. In coming years, as the SPPI and other related initiatives build up their networks, resources and outreach, information on SPP/GPP from other parts of the world will likely surface.

3. Findings

3.1 Definitions and Scope of SPP/GPP

The research focused on "Sustainable Public Procurement" (SPP) activities being undertaken by national governments around the world. Notably, not all stakeholders use the terms "Sustainable Public Procurement" and/or "Green Public Procurement" (SPP/GPP in the report) in the same way or with the exact same definition and scope. In researching material for this report, the related concepts of Environmentally Preferable Procurement (EPP), Socially Responsible Procurement (SRP)[10] and Responsible Purchasing[11] were also included, which cover many of the same concepts.

In some countries, "Sustainable Public Procurement" (SPP) is used, typically incorporating environmental, social and economic aspects while in other countries, "Green Public Procurement" (GPP) is used, indicating a focus on environmental criteria. In this report, the moniker "SPP/GPP" is used throughout to encompass both concepts. In future studies, analyzing how SPP and GPP (and related terms) are used and defined by public entities will help to form a more precise mapping of the extent of their influence over procurement practice.

The definition of 'Sustainable Procurement' adopted by the Marrakech Task Force on Sustainable Public Procurement was:
> "A process whereby organizations meet their needs for goods, services, works and utilities in a way that achieves value for money on a whole life basis in terms of generating benefits not only to the organization, but also to society and the economy, whilst minimising damage to the environment."[12]

In the European Union, Green Public Procurement (GPP) is defined as:
> "A process whereby public authorities seek to procure goods, services and works with a reduced environmental impact throughout their life cycle when compared to goods, services and works with the same primary function that would otherwise be procured."[13]

3.1.1 Common Terms Used for SPP/GPP

A survey question asked respondents about the terms used for SPP/GPP in their country, with the results shown in Figure 5. As the survey was conducted in English and only asked about English-language terms for SPP/GPP, the responses are limited to English terminology.

Green Public Procurement/Purchasing (GPP) and Sustainable Public Procurement/Purchasing (SPP) were the two most popular terms selected by survey respondents; followed by Environmentally Preferable Procurement/Purchasing (EPP).

---

10   The World Bank's SPP Policy is called " Socially Responsible Procurement". See also O. Mont and C. Leire, 2009.

11   "Responsible purchasing or procurement" is oftentimes used in a corporate context, but also sometimes for local government. For example, the City of London's policy on SPP is called "Responsible Procurement Policy" and the USA-based network of State and Local Government SPP practitioners is named the "Responsible Purchasing Network".

12   The original source of this definition was from the UK Sustainable Procurement Task Force Report, 2006.

13   European Commission, 2008.

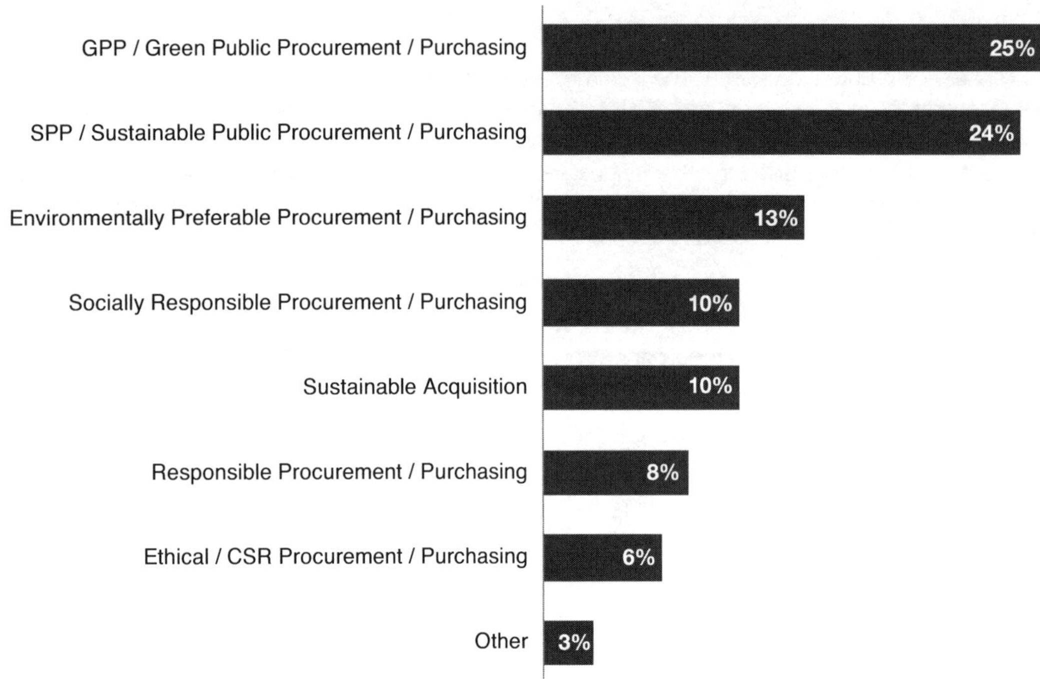

Figure 5: Most commonly used terms for SPP/GPP

EPP is popular in the US, where there was high participation rate for the survey. Other than the options provided, terms mentioned included:

- Green Innovative Procurement
- Eco-Efficiency Measures
- Green Procurement
- Sustainable Purchasing
- Due Process, and
- Sustainable Consumption and Production.

In defining their SPP/GPP policies, strategies and action plans, national governments often create their own definitions and approaches to SPP/GPP. Based on a review of a sample of policies from Europe, North America and Asia, the themes and principles covered oftentimes include:

- Achieving other goals for good procurement practices, including value for money, transparency, fairness, non-discrimination, competition, verifiability and accountability;
- Balancing economic, environmental and social factors when making procurement decisions;
- Generating benefits to society and/or reducing negative social outcomes;
- Generating benefits to the environment and/or reducing environmental impacts;
- Considering the impacts of a product or service being bought over its full life-cycle;
- Seeking resource efficiency and financial savings;
- Helping to optimize costs, including encouraging life cycle costing or whole of life costing methods;
- Improving the quality of products and services available on the market; and
- Demonstrating leadership, and by so doing generating new market opportunities for greener companies, products and services.

SPP/ GPP is also connected to other prevalent procurement concepts. For example, Pablo Prüssing Fuchslocher from Dirección ChileCompra explained that in Chile, "Integrity is the keyword. SPP is about behaving ethically as procurement officers and buyers, understanding the rules, applying the rules in practice."

3.1.2 Environmental and Social Aspects of SPP/GPP

Activities taking place under the umbrella terms of SPP/GPP can vary between those focusing solely on environmental or green aspects; those focusing on social aspects; on economic development aspects or all three. In the survey, government participants were asked which of these aspects their national governments' work on SPP/GPP covers, with results shown in Figure 6. The question was intentionally designed to provide a high-level response to see whether SPP/GPP was typically limited to environmental aspects or whether it was expanded to consider also social and economic aspects per the definition of sustainability.

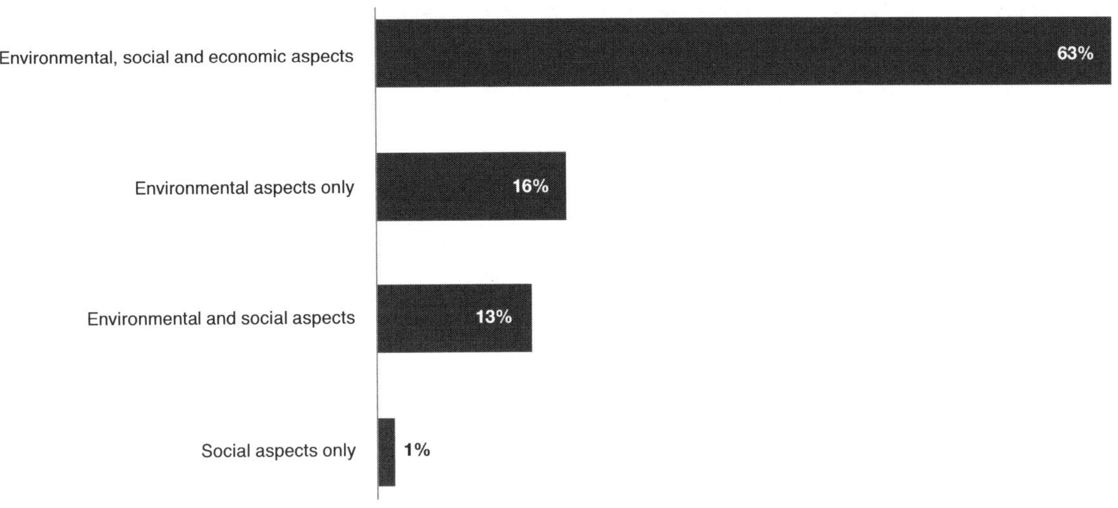

Figure 6: Scope of SPP/GPP work by national governments

The majority of national government respondents were taking a "sustainability" (environmental, social and economic) focus to their SPP/GPP procurement work. This was followed by a group of national governments that are focusing on environmental aspects only. However, a respondent from Lebanon also noted that economic aspects are covered in terms of basic low cost principle (vs. lifecycle cost); and similarly, a respondent from the UK stated that economic aspects are typically covered by "value for money" provisions in all procurement, and are thus not designated as "SPP/GPP" because they are already included. In addition, some respondents commented that without more specificity on what constitutes "social" or "economic" aspects, this was difficult to provide a precise response. For example, one respondent from the USA stated, "…does social aspects include helping small, woman-owned, minority-owned, and/or disabled veteran-owned businesses as part of sustainability? If the answer is yes, then we have many policies".

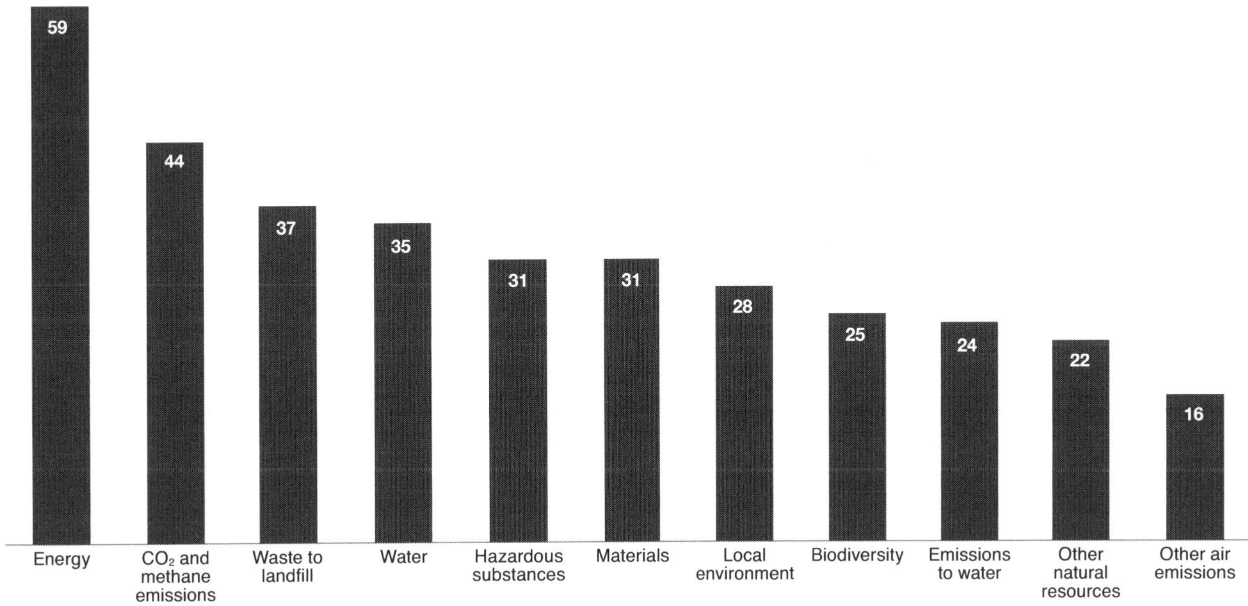

Figure 7: Environmental Aspects cited by national governments as priority

There are many different environmental issues and impacts associated with procurement, however not all are considered priority or are currently covered by SPP/GPP policies. National government respondents were asked whether there were any "priority" environmental issues that were covered by an SPP/GPP policy[14], with results shown in Figure 7.

The environmental aspect most often mentioned was "energy" followed by "CO_2 and methane emissions" then "waste to landfill" as a priority. All of the environmental aspects provided as an option were selected as a response by at least one respondent. On average five aspects were selected, so it appears that SPP/GPP typically goes beyond any one single environmental attribute. Some respondents indicated that environmental priorities are determined by product category and cannot be generalized across all categories or sectors in their country.

A similar question was posed to national government respondents as to the social aspects considered priority in their country's SPP/GPP policies, with responses shown in Figure 8.

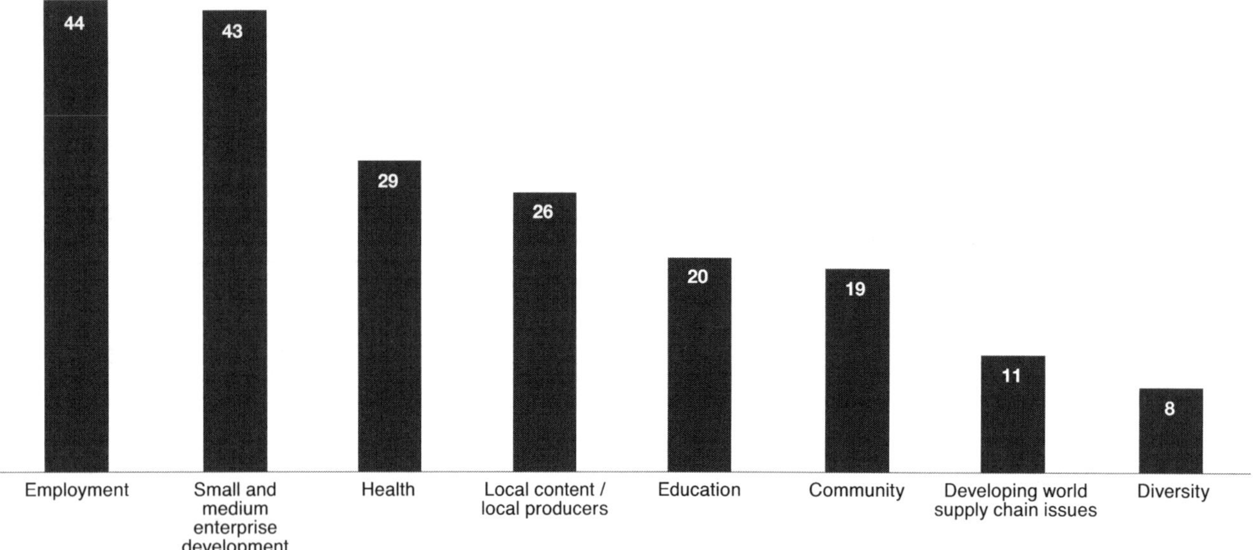

Figure 8: Social Aspects cited by national governments as priority

The most mentioned social aspect by respondents was "employment", followed by "small and medium enterprise development", then "health". Respondents on average selected three social aspects. Those who noted "other" social aspects mentioned "employment of disabled staff", "gender equity" and "human rights". The research suggests that environmental aspects tend to be focused on the product level, while social aspects are identified primarily at the company level. This reflects the notion that social issues are often located at the facility or supplier level rather than at the product level.

3.2 Regulations and Policies on SPP/GPP

In different countries, policies on SPP/GPP range from top-down decrees and executive orders, to SPP/GPP-specific national action plans, to provisions embedded within procurement policies and regulations. In this report an inclusive approach to the definition of what is an "SPP/GPP policy" was taken in order to map the different types of policy approaches being taken.

This section first provides an overview of the different legal and policy frameworks for SPP/GPP being employed (in international and national contexts) then provides an overview of the array of different legal and policy approaches being taken in different countries.

---

14   Environmental and social aspect categories used in the survey were provided by UNEP, and were based the report "Procuring the Future", UK Sustainable Procurement Task Force (2006).

3.2.1 Legal and Regulatory Framework

Figure 9 provides an overview of the different international, regional, national and sub-national regulatory and policy frameworks of relevance to SPP/GPP.

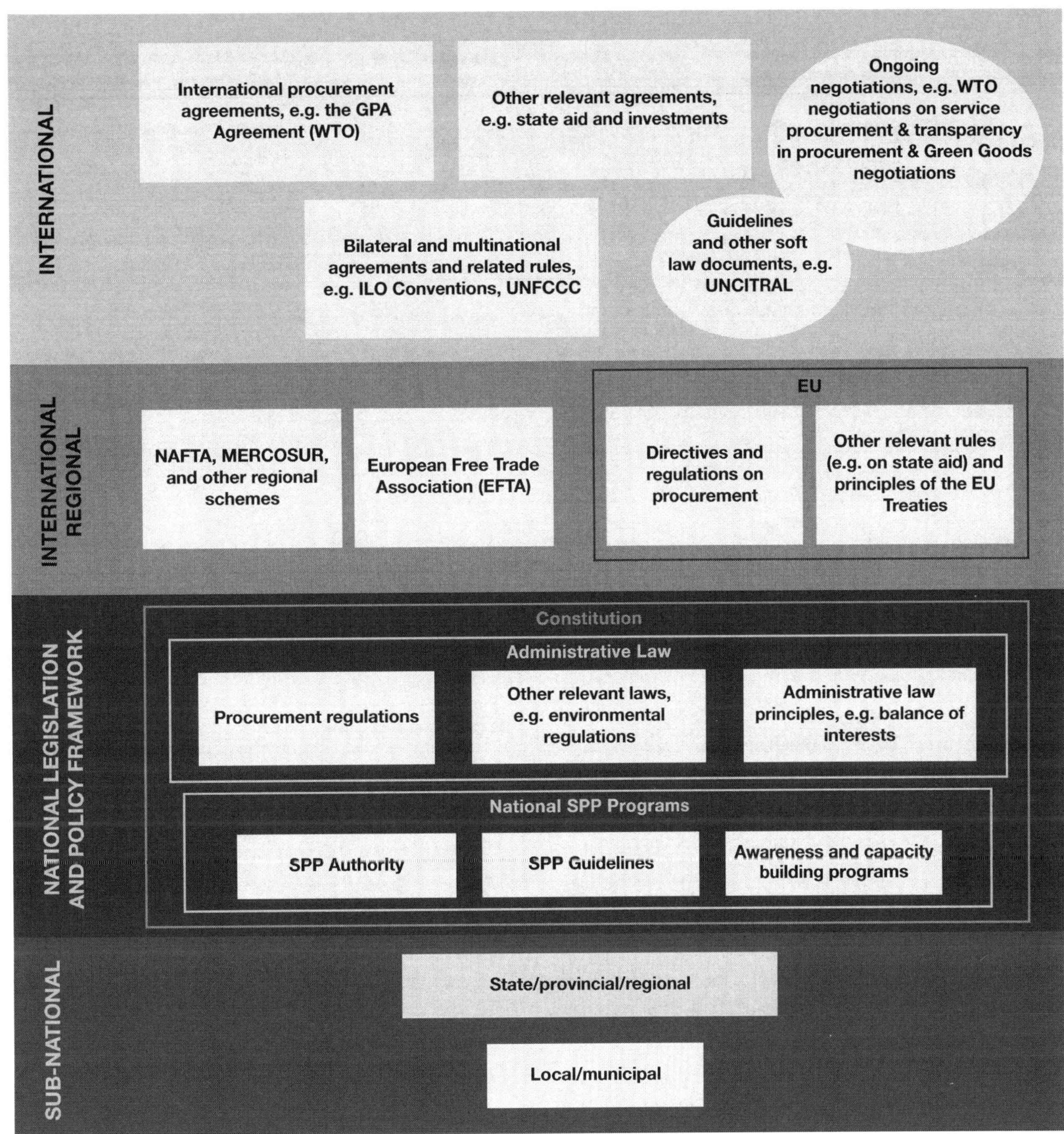

Figure 9: The international, regional and national legal frameworks for SPP/GPP

For most countries, public procurement is influenced by national and international legal frameworks such as the Government Procurement Agreement (GPA)[15] from the World Trade Organization (WTO), or the United Nations Commission on International Trade Law's (UNCITRAL) model law. Public procurement guidelines developed by the World Bank or development finance institutions, including multilateral regional development banks are also increasingly influential. International Labour Organization (ILO) Conventions and multi-lateral environmental agreements such as the United Nations Framework Convention on Climate Change (UNFCCC) also drive policy commitments and in some cases, regulation.

---

15   WTO GPA is a voluntary plurilateral reciprocal agreement that establishes rules for tendering and requires fairness, and which is intended to make government procurement markets less discriminatory and more transparent. Furthermore, public procurement guidelines developed by the World Bank or development finance institutions, including multilateral regional development banks, are becoming increasingly important.

Regional and inter-governmental directives can require or encourage the adoption of action plans or mandates on SPP/GPP. For example, OECD member country governments have agreed on a Council Recommendation "to improve the environmental performance of public procurement" that formalises the declaration of support for the use of environmentally-preferable public procurement practices expressed in the OECD Environmental Strategy for the First Decade of the 21st Century, adopted by OECD Environment Ministers in May 2001.[16]

Inter-governmental economic agreements like the economic and political agreement MERCOSUR[17] or free trade agreements such as NAFTA structure the types of provisions that may be included in a national SPP/GPP law or policy.

In the EU, GPP is governed by the EU Public Procurement Directives which are then transposed in national legislations. The Member States at the national government level are required to adhere to sector-specific EU laws and to act upon mandatory GPP requirements on vehicles, energy performance of buildings, timber and information technology (IT) equipment (under ENERGY STAR). Definitions and verification techniques are also provided for renewable energy and organic food, however their purchase is not required. The EU GPP legislative framework is one of the most elaborate in the world and is described in further detail in the case study provided in Appendix 1.[18]

National legal and regulatory frameworks include constitutional and/or administrative laws. Constitutional norms may include:

- Environmental protection or social constitutional goals
- Relevant constitutional and/or administrative law concepts
- Rules of behaviour concerning the administration
- The definition of public interests, and
- National procurement laws.

While different ministries are behind the implementation of these laws, typically Ministries of the Environment and/or Commerce/Industry are responsible for them. In some countries, public procurement authorities (usually under Ministries of Finance) are in charge of developing public procurement legislation and acts. The extent to which SPP/GPP is integrated into the core public procurement legal or regulatory structure, a concept lately referred to as "mainstreaming" SPP/GPP, will likely affect the outcomes of practices.[19]

3.2.2 National SPP/GPP Policy Adoption

Sustainability considerations came to the policy agenda for many countries in the mid-1990s, catalysed in part by Agenda 21 that was adopted in Rio in 1992.[20] At this time, many countries, regions or local governments took a first step towards adopting SPP/GPP policies. By 2000, a number of OECD countries had in place or were developing SPP/GPP guidelines. This activity was partly in response to Chapter III of the Johannesburg Plan of Implementation adopted at the World Summit on Sustainable Development in 2002, where SPP/GPP was featured as one of the means to achieve sustainability. The outcome document of the 2012 United Nations Conference on Sustainable Development (Rio+20) adopted the 10-Year Framework of Programmes on Sustainable Consumption and Production.[21] Sustainable public procurement is listed as one of the five initial sustainable consumption and production programmes proposed for development.[22] This renewed commitment should continue to drive countries to adopt SPP/GPP policies and practices.

Most OECD countries now have a national SPP/GPP policy or program in place.[23] Brazil and China have developed national legal frameworks on SPP/GPP. Russia is yet to develop such a program, and it currently focuses on timber production and the implementation of the regional product standard "GOST R".[24]

Until recently, national SPP/GPP policies and programs in developing and emerging countries have been few.[25] In India, public procurement legislation is being revised and will include a provision for GPP accompanied by guidelines (see Appendix 1 case study on India). In South Africa, procurement is used as an environmental policy tool to contribute to

---

16   OCED 2002a.

17   www.mercosurtc.com

18   http://ec.europa.eu/environment/gpp/eu_public_directives_en.htm

19   TemaNord, 2012.

20   In Chapter 4 of Agenda 21 document of the UN Global Environment Conference emphasizes the importance that state contracts set an example in environmental respect.

21   Paragraph 226 of document A/CONF.216/L.1 – The Future We Want.

22   Paragraph 8 of document A/CONF.216/5.

23   Oshani et al., 2007.

24   http://www.gost-r.info/

25   Oshani et al. ,2007.

sustainable development while also addressing past discriminatory policies and practices.[26] In the last five years, an increasing number of countries have adopted SPP/GPP policies, including Bulgaria, Chile, Costa Rica, Colombia, Israel, Lebanon, Mauritius, Romania, Tunisia and Slovenia.

Of the 62 countries with national government respondents participating in the survey, some 43 indicated that a national institution has adopted a SPP/GPP policy. Through additional research, a further 11 countries were identified as having adopted a national SPP/GPP policy, and several more are in the process of developing and/or adopting policies. Importantly, not all national SPP/GPP policies take the same form: there are National Action Plans, Executive Orders, Decrees, and/or sustainability-related requirements within national procurement policies and regulations. Due to the volunteer reporting that is the basis of the survey sample for this study, it is difficult to draw absolute conclusions on the coverage and development of national policies in a global context. However, the results reveal a useful picture of the number and variations of types of policies now in place for SPP/GPP at a national level.

The regional spread of the national policies found in the survey and with additional research included:

- **Asia**: Seven countries participating in the survey reported the existence of a national policy on SPP/GPP. Desktop research found an additional three Asian countries have a national SPP/GPP policy adopted (China, Israel and Japan);

- **Africa**: Seven countries participating in the survey reported the existence of a national policy on SPP/GPP. Desktop research found one additional country with a national SPP/GPP policy adopted (Ghana);

- **Europe**: Twenty countries participating in the survey reported the existence of a national policy on SPP/GPP, typically in the form of a National Action Plan. Desktop research and a EU 2012 report[27] found an additional five countries with a National Action Plan, bringing the European total to 25 countries. The same EU report also identified four more countries currently working on their National Action Plans for GPP (Greece, Hungary, Ireland and Romania);

- **Latin America and the Caribbean**: Eight countries reported the existence of a national policy on SPP/GPP in the survey. Desktop research found one additional country (Uruguay) with a national SPP/GPP policy adopted;

- **North America**: One country reported a national policy on SPP/GPP in the survey (USA). Desktop research found one country (Canada) adopted a national SPP/GPP policy in 2006, bringing the North American total to two; and

- **Oceania**: No countries participated in the survey. However, desktop research found that both Australia and New Zealand have a national SPP/GPP policy in place.

In sum, the survey combined with desktop research estimates that by the end of 2012, at least 56 countries had adopted a national SPP/GPP policy in some form.

The region with the largest number of national SPP/GPP policies adopted by national governments was Europe, showing the influence of the EU Directives on GPP and OECD recommendations.

Interestingly, there were some differences of opinion by respondents from the same country as to whether or not they had adopted national SPP/GPP policy. When checked, the reason for the different reply came down to how "policy" was defined, and what could be considered as being ultimately "adopted" and by which ministry or agency.

Non-national government stakeholders were asked the same question (as to whether there was a national government policy adopted on SPP/GPP in their country). Comparing their responses to those of national government representatives, more discrepancies were found. In several cases, the national government representative indicated the existence of a national government policy while the non-national government stakeholder said there was no policy and vice versa. This points to the need for governments to improve their communications and awareness-raising on SPP/GPP policies both internally to government agency representatives, as well as more broadly to other stakeholder groups in their region. It also points to the need for a more refined measure of an "adopted SPP/GPP policy".

National government respondents were also asked the year in which their national SPP/GPP policy was first adopted, with results shown in Figure 10.

The survey results show that there has been an increase in national government policy activity on SPP/GPP in the last five years, going back to at least 1995. The rise in adoption of GPP/SPP policies seen in 2007 all occurred in European Countries, presumably following the GPP guidance and public procurement directives provided by the European Union.

---

26   Bolton, 2009, cited in in Ho, 2010.
27   EC August 2012 http://ec.europa.eu/environment/gpp/pdf/national_gpp_strategies_en.pdf.

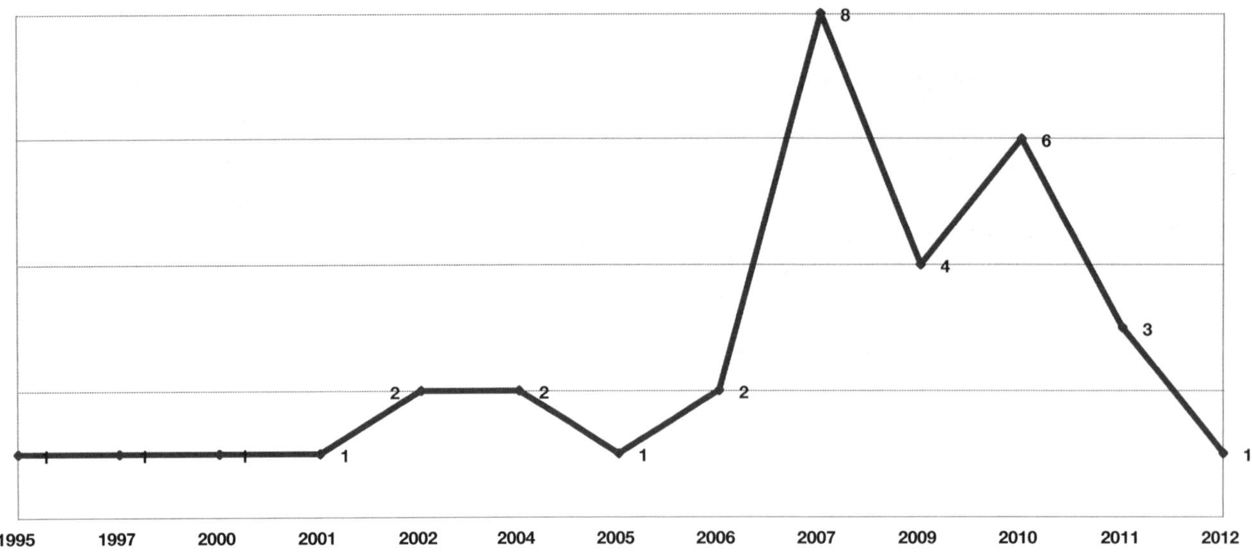

Figure 10: The year that national SPP/GPP policies were adopted by those countries surveyed

3.2.3 The Integration of SPP/GPP in Provisions into Other Policies and Regulations

SPP/GPP provisions are not only found in national policies dedicated to the topic, oftentimes provisions for SPP/GPP are embedded in other regulations and policies.

National governments survey respondents were asked to nominate in what types of policy are SPP/GPP provisions currently found, with results shown in Figure 11.

The results indicate that most often, SPP/GPP provisions are embedded within procurement policy and regulations, ahead of dedicated national SPP/GPP action plans. There is no single policy arena that dominates; indeed, several respondents noted that SPP/GPP provisions could be found in several of different places in their country. Another respondent noted that that there is significant overlap between SCP policy, sustainable development strategy and green economy.

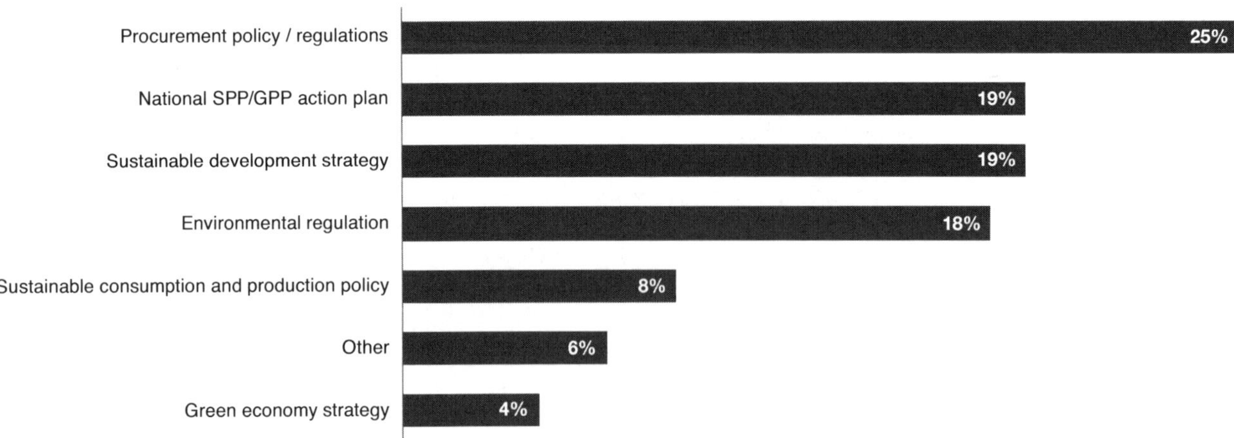

Figure 11: Policy arenas where SPP/GPP policies are currently found

3.2.4 Approaches to SPP/GPP Policy Development

A range of approaches to the development of SPP/GPP policy exist today, reflecting differences in existing political infrastructures and policy processes.[28] There are different pathways towards developing SPP/GPP policy, with some favouring more top-down processes and others favouring bottom-up approaches.[29] Others argue that a so-called "sandwich structure" of top-down and bottom-up initiatives is the most effective approach, and it has been claimed that European national initiatives often are driven this way.[30] For example, in Nordic countries, SPP/GPP instruments are used at different levels and are designed to be complementary.[31] An OECD study[32] from 2007 suggests that although a number of OECD countries do not have SPP/GPP integrated into the law, their public sectors nevertheless implement SPP/GPP practices.

Oftentimes the structure used to promote SPP/GPP reflects the types of agencies involved in SPP/GPP policy and implementation. National government respondents were asked in the survey what agencies are playing a leading and important role in SPP/GPP in their country, with results shown in Figure 12.

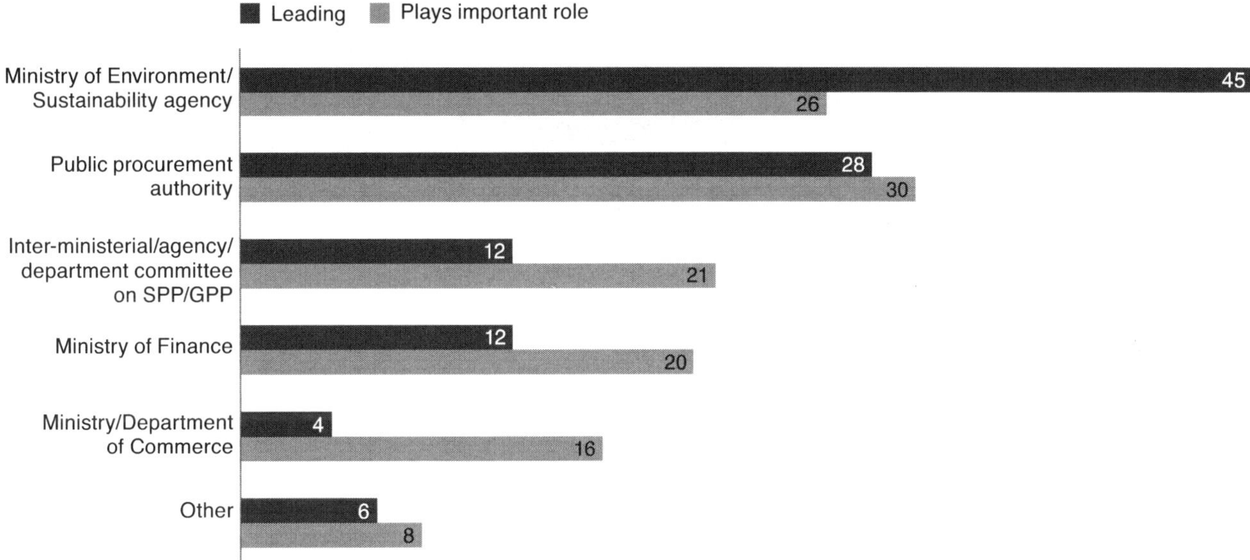

Figure 12: National agencies involved in SPP/GPP

The national agencies involved in SPP/GPP were spread out, with no single agency dominating. The type of agency cited most often as playing a "leading" role in SPP/GPP was ministries of environment/sustainability. Public procurement agencies were either playing a leading or supporting role, and ministries of finance and commerce were most often playing a supporting role in SPP/GPP implementation. Inter-ministerial committees on SPP/GPP were selected as leading or playing an important role by 33 respondents — such committee are recommended to be formed in the UNEP SPP Guidelines to enable effective implementation.[33] Abby Semple, an SPP expert based in the United Kingdom (UK) observed, "there is a risk that if the SPP policy is too high-level and is not developed together with procurement practitioners, people don't take it seriously and it doesn't get done".

Other functions mentioned by respondents as playing an important role in SPP/GPP in their country included Presidential Councils (e.g. The White House Council on Environmental Quality in the USA); the Ministry of Energy, Green Technology and Water (Malaysia), Department of Planning (Columbia), the Ministry of National Development (Hungary) and an NGO that is supported also by UNDP and UNEP (Cegesti, Costa Rica).

In Japan, the 2000 "Law on Promoting Green Purchasing" makes it mandatory for government institutions to implement green procurement, while encouraging local authorities, private companies and individuals to make efforts for procuring environmentally sound products and services. In Denmark, the central government requires public bodies to develop green procurement policies. In the UK, the government mandates the use of buying standards for central government procurement. In Australia and New Zealand, the "Government Framework for Sustainable Procurement" provides a set of principles to guide federal, state, and territory governments.[34]

28　Thomson & Jackson, 2007.
29　ITPS, 2006.
30　Steurer et al., 2007.
31　Bauer et al., 2009.
32　OECD, 2007.
33　UNEP, 2012
34　Eco-Buy, 2009.

While a mandatory approach appeals for its apparent simplicity, there are some reservations. One interviewee explained, "with mandatory approaches to GPP, you can end-up with lowest-common-denominator criteria. You also require proper reporting and monitoring systems, and I don't believe we are there yet".

The extent to which mandatory SPP/GPP policy at the national level applies only to national government agencies, or also to other state and local government entities varies depending on the institutional configuration of government in different countries, and the extent to which national governments can mandate any policies to other levels of government. National government respondents were asked in the survey what level of government was covered by any mandatory SPP/GPP policies in place, with results shown in Figure 13.

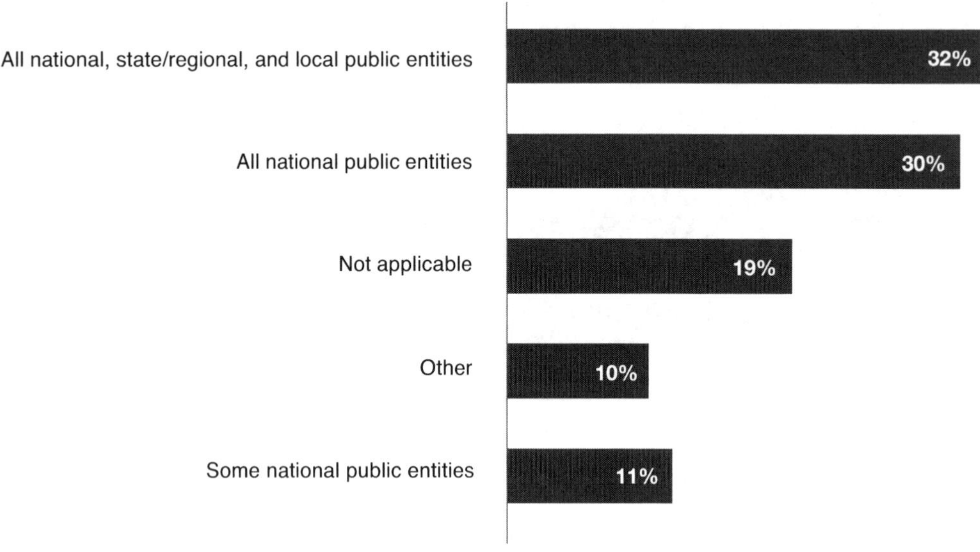

Figure 13: Level of government agencies covered by mandatory SPP/GPP policies (where mandatory policies are present)

The survey results show that countries tend to either mandate SPP/GPP all the way down to the local level, or their policies remain at the national level. A smaller number cover some but not all national agencies, and a large proportion indicate that the question was "not applicable" in that they did not have any mandatory SPP/GPP requirements.

In Japan, all central government ministries practice green procurement; all 47 prefectural governments and 12 designated cities are engaged in green procurement, and two-thirds of the 700 cities now systematically implement green procurement (see the Case Study on Japan in Appendix 1).

In some countries, SPP/GPP policies are mandatory for some product categories but not others. For example, in Portugal, Germany, and the Czech Republic, GPP is legally binding for some product groups.[35] Denmark, France, the Netherlands, and the UK have public procurement policies specifically for wood and paper products. In Belgium, there is an initiative to ensure that 50 per cent of government vehicles comply with specific environmental criteria.[36] In Ecuador, Decree 1883/2009 requires state agencies to purchase fuel-efficient and/or hybrid vehicles.

Different regulatory and policy regimes allow for different scope of criteria that can be applied to product-related criteria only, to product and process criteria; or to product, process and producer criteria. The WTO non-discrimination discipline[37] should be carefully considered, in that product or service standards are permitted to differentiate between "like" products; and non-product related processes and production methods (PPMs) are allowed[38] if the conditions made are considered "necessary to...protect human, animal or plant life or health".[39] Recently adopted text by the WTO allows environmental criteria to be used in technical specifications and evaluation criteria.[40]

---

35   European Commission, 2010.

36   Steurer et al., 2007.

37   WTO (1947) GATT, Articles I and III, and WTO (2011) GPA, Article III.

38   WTO, 2011, See also: Oshani et al., 2007.

39   WTO (1947) GPA, Article XXIII.

40   WTO, 12 April 2012, Committee on Government Procurement: 12-1744, Article VI: states that "For greater certainty, a Party, including its procuring entities, may, in accordance with this Article, prepare, adopt or apply technical specifications to promote the conservation of natural resources or protect the environment." (p20).

According to the EU Procurement Directives, production characteristics should be considered equivalent to performance characteristics — the award criteria must be related to the "subject matter" in the contract, i.e. the product or the service, and not the supplier as such.[41] Many hope that the revised EU Procurement Directives will allow for clearly defined "production characteristics" and clarify that production characteristics can and should be included as technical specifications and award criteria.[42] New EU Directives are expected that will incorporate stronger guidance on life cycle costing in procurement.[43]

3.2.5 The Use of Targets

A number of public institutions have set ambitious targets for SPP/GPP implementation. National government survey respondents were asked whether there were any targets in place for national governments on SPP/GPP today, with results shown in Figure 14.

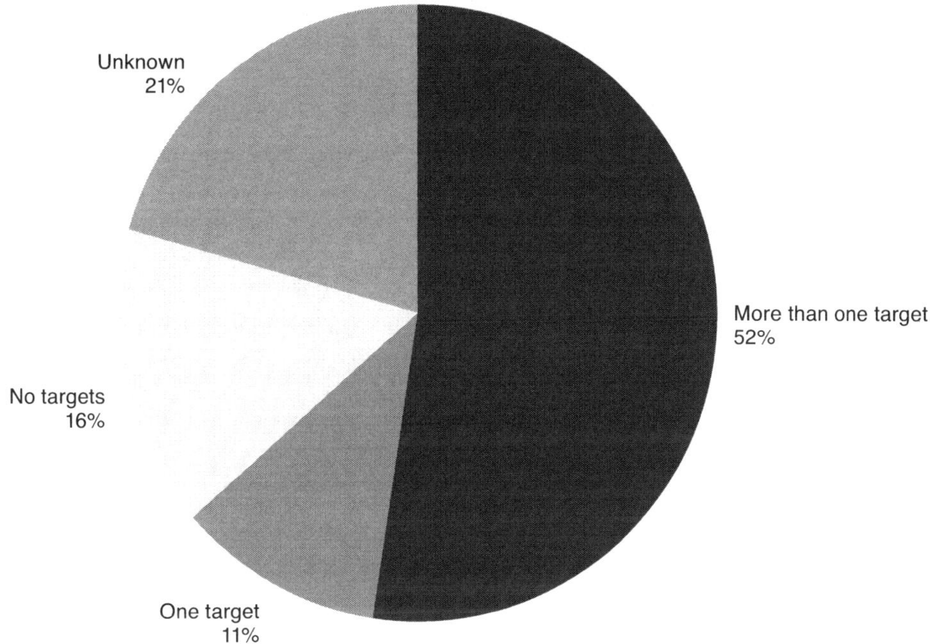

Figure 14: The use of targets for SPP/GPP by national governments

Forty-three countries (55 per cent of those responding to the question) have either a single SPP/GPP target or multiple targets in place.

The type of targets being set varies considerably. Some countries use quantitative targets/goals, such as a percentage of all procurement to meet certain criteria by a certain year. Others establish programmatic goals, such as "implementing the SPP/GPP policy".

Some targets are currently under revision or will be revised in the near future. For example, a respondent from the Netherlands noted that even though they were successful in meeting their ambitious targets, they are now moving away from setting quantitative targets given difficulties and costs involved with monitoring the activities precisely. Instead, they are considering introducing a more qualitative measurement that includes other aspects such as innovative procurement and the use of award criteria. An interviewee for this study commented that mandates and targets need to be "ambitious yet realistic", and that they should be accompanied by monitoring or risk remaining "in name only".

Even if targets are set or even mandated, monitoring and reporting of SPP/GPP activities is often not mandatory and continues to be problematic. Japan and Sweden are exceptions, requiring all state ministries, departments and agencies to define procurement targets every fiscal year and make the results of GPP efforts publicly available. In Sweden, the use of the national GPP tool is reported to the government on a continuous basis.

---

41 Michelsen & de Boer, 2009.
42 ENDS Europe, 2012.
43 Misiga, 2011.

3.2.6 Complementary Sustainable Consumption and Production (SCP) Policies

Green product standards and ecolabels can help to facilitate national SPP/GPP policy and implementation, whether these standards and ecolabels are directly supported by national governments or recognised by them for their procurement. Without credible standards that determine what products count as green or sustainable, governments find it difficult to implement SPP/GPP. Indeed it has been established that ecolabels play an important role in helping the application of SPP/GPP practices[44] and studies on the EU have shown that the uptake of SPP/GPP strongly correlates to the existence of an ecolabel scheme.[45] The similarity of SPP/GPP criteria for some product groups among many European countries has been attributed to the use of established ecolabels in that region.[46]

Alison Kinn Bennett of the US EPA explained the importance of ecolabels and standards to policy-makers, "In the US, it's been very important for government officials to both participate in the development of and use consensus-based sustainability standards in procurement. This leads to more robust sustainability criteria in key procurement categories and ensures some market alignment around greener options. Otherwise, government and industry may not be on the same page, leading to market confusion and products and services that don't meet our needs." Alenka Burja of the Ministry of Agriculture and Environment in Slovenia explained that, "verification is very important to GPP. But while ecolabels are the easiest way to set criteria and verify claims, there are currently not enough product categories covered by them, and not enough products with the labels. Therefore, more emphasis on cleaner production methods and better products is also needed."

China and Thailand also have their own ecolabel schemes and are supporting them through public procurement.[47] In 2007, the Chinese central and provincial governments were asked to give priority to environment-friendly products listed in a "green product inventory". The list included products ranging from cars to construction materials that have been approved by the China Certification Committee for Environmental Labelling. A challenge faced by developing countries is the lack of reliable standards and ecolabels; and also lack of products that have been certified to those that do exist. Augustine Koh from the Green Purchasing Network in Malaysia cautioned that, "Everybody is talking green now, but the number of products certified to credible ecolabels is so small we can't just specify those — not until industry has caught up and there are many more green products to buy."

As discussed in section 3.3.4, standards and ecolabels are needed to identify the most sustainable products. There also have to be enough products meeting those standards for governments to specify them, especially given the large scale of their procurement activity. The focus on green market development by governments within the SPP/GPP context is visible in some countries. For example, Malaysia, the Republic of Korea, Thailand and China have been using a variety of mechanisms to stimulate green products and the growth of green industries. Japan has long pushed to increase the supply of green products. Its "2001 Green Purchasing Law" focused on providing the tools and methods by which Japan could become a "recycling-based society" through promoting green procurement and providing information on environmentally friendly products in a central database administered by the Japanese Green Purchasing Network.

3.2.7 Discussion of Policy Findings

The overall policy and procurement environment has a substantial influence on how SPP/GPP is addressed by policy.[48] For example, many countries are now decentralizing their public procurement. This offers new opportunities to try out different approaches in different regions. For example in the UK, Wales has piloted maximising procurement from SMEs by adding social clauses, and Scotland has set demanding targets for renewable energy use.[49]

Another critical point is to have sufficient support and involvement by the relevant ministries and agencies in proposing, adopting and implementing SPP/GPP policies. The survey showed that both environmental and procurement agencies are playing leading and important roles in their countries, and it may even be argued that involvement by both types of agencies are needed. If not, the risk is that the work of individual ministries is inadequately integrated and/or that policies don't correspond to the reality of procurement processes. In many countries, the environmental ministry may have a mandate to implement SPP/GPP, but there is a disconnect between this mandate and what the trade or finance ministry is doing. As one interviewee described, "Policy people often don't understand procurement, and don't understand why it's hard to get it right. Therefore it has to be the right kind of policy and with the right ministries supporting it or it gets ignored".

---

44   Norden, 2011.
45   Rabbiosi, 2010.
46   AEA Techology, 2010.
47   Environment Development Centre, 2008; Global Ecolabelling Network (GEN) AGM, 2009.
48   Brammer & Walker, 2010.
49   Thomson & Jackson, 2007.

High-level recognition of the importance of SPP/GPP by top policy makers/regulators is often argued to be the most important driver for SPP/GPP. Answers to the survey on drivers certainly supports this view (Section 3.5). Procurers and decision-makers need mandates to make changes and to be clear on the international and national legal framework in which they are operating. Mats Ekenger of the Nordic Council of Ministers remarked, "you come to a point when the studies, projects and discussions become counter-productive because too much time has passed. Then you need legislation to move forward".

However, a less specific national legal framework can also be used to the advantage of the initial SPP/GPP developments. As observed by Pablo Prüssing Fuchslocher from Dirección ChileCompra, "as long as the law is "open" then you can include SPP/GPP, and it might get implemented faster. If you have to get it through congress or parliament, it will take forever and may just hold things up."

In some cases, countries are pushing the boundaries on what is currently legally allowed in order to implement SPP/GPP. It has later turned out that this has been an effective form of leadership on SPP/GPP.

3.3 Implementation of SPP/GPP Practices

Five years ago, IISD reported that there was little published information on SPP/GPP implementation. Today, there is both more implementation activity internationally, and more information being reported about it.

It may be the case that there are more implementation activities being undertaken than there are formal national policies and regulations. In addition, because some greener or more sustainable products may not be designated clearly as such, there may actually be more SPP/GPP activity than is reported.

This section first provides an indication of the set of countries currently seen as SPP/GPP leaders and innovators by survey stakeholders. It then provides an overview of the different implementation activities being undertaken by national governments, and explores the use of some of the different tools such as product guidelines, ecolabels and life cycle costing that enable implementation.

3.3.1 Perceived Leaders in SPP/GPP Implementation

The extent and nature of SPP/GPP implementation practices varies significantly across regions.[50] Most OECD countries have now undertaken some form of activity, and it is generally agreed[51] that the frontrunners within this segment are Japan, the US, Canada and the European so-called "Green-7" countries (Austria, Denmark, Finland, Germany, the Netherlands, Sweden and the UK[52]), as well as Belgium, Italy and Spain.

Stakeholder survey respondents were asked to nominate the countries that they consider are advanced and/or innovative in SPP/GPP[53], with results shown in Tables 1 and 2 (next page).

---

50   Brammer & Walker, 2010.

51   Oshani et al., 2007.

52   According to literature as well as a number of consultations with SPP experts. See PricewaterhouseCoopers (PwC), Significant and Ecofys, 2009.

53   The survey questions read "What three countries would you say are the most advanced in terms of SPP/GPP implementation?" and "Aside from those countries you selected in the last question, what countries are doing interesting, unique or innovative work on SPP/GPP? Please nominate countries and explain why."

Countries cited as leading (number of mentions)	
1	Sweden (40)
2	United Kingdom (39)
3	Germany (37)
4	Denmark (23)
5	Switzerland (22)
6	Japan (21)
7	Netherlands (18)
8	United States of America (18)
9	Norway (16)
10	Canada (12)
11	France (11)
12	Republic of Korea (10)
13	Austria (8)
14	Australia (5)
15	Brazil (5)

Table 1: Countries cited as leading in SPP/GPP

Cited as most innovative (number of mentions)	
1	United States of America (16)
2	Brazil (14)
3	UK (11)
4	China (10)
5	France (9)
6	Germany (9)
7	Italy (9)
8	Spain (9)
9	Costa Rica (8)
10	Canada (6)
11	Denmark (6)
12	Finland (6)
13	Japan (6)
14	Republic of Korea (6)
15	Sweden (6)

Table 2: Countries cited as innovative in SPP/GPP

A total of 40 different countries were selected as being 'most advanced' in SPP/GPP, however as many respondents selected their own countries as leaders, these results are somewhat biased. The "Green-7" in the EU are well represented in this list, with the exception of Finland. For those cited as doing interesting, unique or innovative work on SPP/GPP, some 54 countries, cities and/or regions were selected. Some illustrative examples of why a particular country or region was chosen by survey respondents are provided in Table 3.

City/Region/Country nominated as innovative	Explanation provided by survey respondents
City of Vienna	Developed a catalogue on SPP/GPP products.
City of Sao Paulo	Information technology systems for public procurement. Service contracts are "virtualized" and GPP products are identified with a state ecolabel.
Chile	Has a unified public procurement platform where SPP/GPP can be implemented efficiently.
China	Central and provincial governments have begun giving priority to products listed in a "green product inventory".
Costa Rica	Has a national action plan, guidelines, and provides several examples of products and services that have been purchased through an SPP/GPP approach.
Denmark	Is applying innovative legal frameworks to further improve the percentage of overall SPP/GPP. Is working on operationalizing life cycle costing.
Germany	Has strong political drivers, national guidelines and programmes for SPP/GPP; public information resources via websites and ecolabels; use of innovative tools like life cycle thinking and green contract variants.
Ghana	The first African country to implement a fully-fledged SPP/GPP policy.
Japan	Has a very rigorous green building code with stringent product requirements.
Netherlands	100 per cent sustainable acquisition target for government institutions.
Spain	Has a National Action Plan; inclusion of GPP in the Public Contract Law; training and resources for GPP in the Basque Country (ihobe - a public body exemplary for market consultations); GPP guidelines in Madrid City; GPP Manual in the Catalan Government.
Sweden	Working on integrating life cycle costing across the board.
United Kingdom	Developed a standard for sustainable procurement (BS 8903:2010).

Table 3: Examples of innovative SPP/GPP work being undertaken by countries/regions/cities as nominated by survey respondents

In the past five years, many countries also began implementing SPP/GPP. Countries such as Chile, Portugal and Bulgaria benefitted from new e-procurement platforms that enable SPP/GPP and greater transparency on procurement practices. E-procurement refers to organizational (public or private) transactions of goods and services over the Internet, and can facilitate the implementation of SPP/GPP by providing a central hub for disseminating information, enforcing preferred supplier and product purchases, and maintaining visibility and control.[54]

Stakeholder survey respondents were also asked to characterise the "extent of SPP/GPP implementation" they see in their country by national governments, with results shown in Figure 15.

Almost 40 per cent of stakeholders thought their governments were "integrating SPP/GPP into procurement in some product categories, but not for others"; and 21 per cent indicated that their governments are "just beginning to design SPP/GPP policies". Only 4 per cent of respondents considered that there is full integration and monitoring of SPP/GPP (in Belgium, Japan, Republic of Tanzania, USA and Viet Nam). These findings indicate that national governments still have work to do to fully implement SPP/GPP comprehensively.

---

54   Dimension Data, 2011.

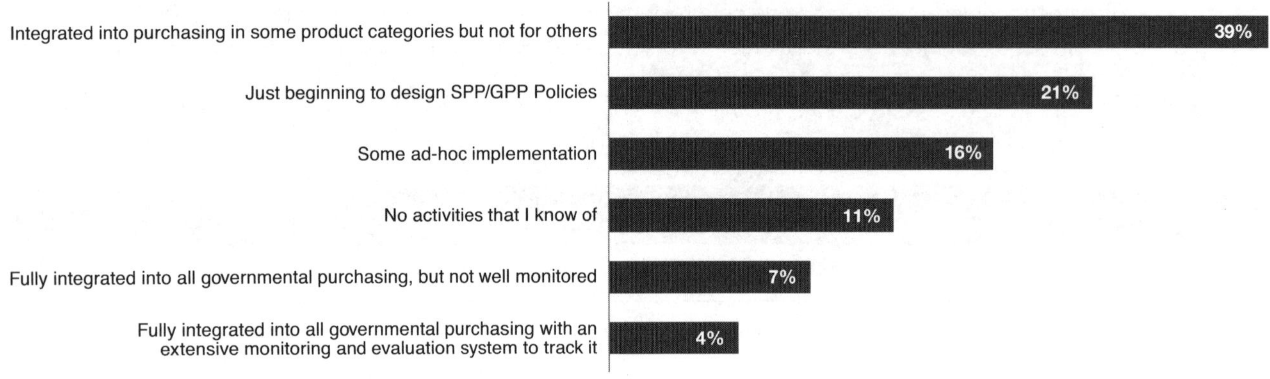

Figure 15: How national governments' implementation on SPP/GPP is being perceived

3.3.2 Overview of SPP/GPP Implementation Activities

Sustainability criteria can shape nearly every stage of the procurement process. Whilst different countries may have different procurement terminology, the procedures and stages in procurement cycles are often similar; a typical procurement cycle is illustrated in Figure 16. In what follows, examples of different SPP/GPP procurement activities are provided throughout the different procurement process phases.

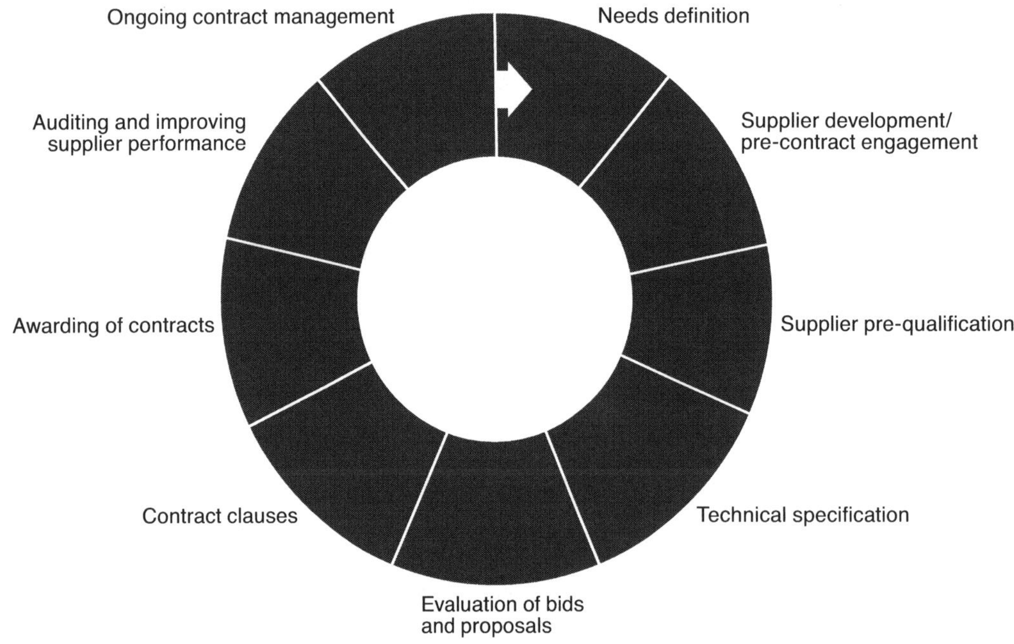

Figure 16: The typical procurement cycle

Optimally, the incorporation of environmental criteria in public procurement should be underpinned with a gradual and structured approach. A careful selection of criteria that are based in accordance with the legal and SCP policy framework is required, and the availability of supply of green products assessed. The latter process should take into consideration the full lifecycle environmental and social aspects of the product or service, focusing on those product categories with the largest impacts. Life Cycle Costing (LCC) or similar techniques can be used to consider the financial dimensions of the provision, and a monitoring system is created to track the results.

In reality, most countries enter SPP/GPP at different starting points and are much less structured and systematic in establishing their programmes. Some focus on the so-called "quick win" products (those products for which it is relatively easy to determine the more sustainable option, and for which contracting procedures are straightforward). Others have followed the structured procedures provided by guidance documents and training such as by the UNEP SPP Approach, derived from the Marrakech Task Force Approach to SPP, and the EU Buy Green Handbook.[55] For example, recent SPP/GPP initiatives in Latin American and Caribbean countries have ensured participation from key stakeholders.[56] In Japan, Sweden and Germany, the greening of products and public procurement started with local initiatives that then expanded nationally. For other countries it is an iterative process.

National government respondents were asked to nominate those SPP/GPP implementation activities they had either completed or were in the process of completing, with the results shown in Figure 17.

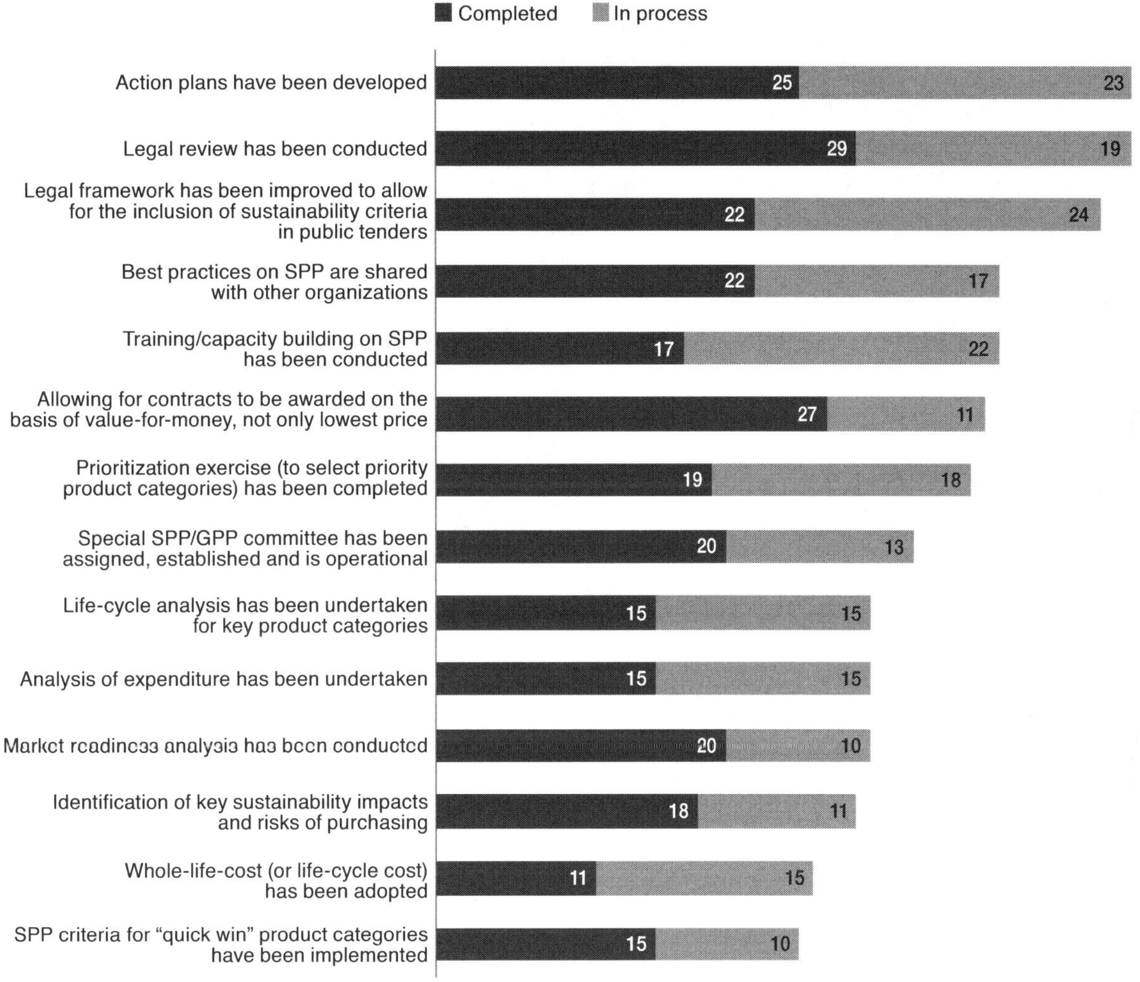

Figure 17: National government SPP/GPP activities either completed or in process

The most common activity completed was the completion of a legal review, followed by allowing for contracts to be awarded based on "value for money" not lowest price. In countries where public procurement reform is taking place, a legal review provides an excellent opportunity to introduce sustainability considerations at an early stage.[57]

The activity most commonly cited as "in process" was improving the legal framework to allow for the inclusion of sustainability criteria, followed by the adoption of national action plans. Other activities mentioned by respondents included: the development of a "Help Desk" for SPP/GPP practitioners, knowledge sharing, and reporting to a central agency. One respondent from the USA commented that their answer would have been different for different federal agencies, as many are taking their own approach.

---

55   Structured approaches are offered by e.g. UNEP, 2012: European Commission, 2004c; Nachhaltige Kompass, 2012 and others. See list of international programmes and initiatives in Appendix 2.

56   Beláustegui, 2011

57   UNEP, 2012.

3.3.3 Integration of SPP/GPP Provisions in the Procurement Cycle

SPP/GPP requirements can be included at different stages in the procurement process, from technical specifications in tender announcements, to award criteria in the final selection of tender, and contract criteria for the completion of the delivery/service. The implementation of GPP/SPP can be measured by procurements practices in one or more stages of the procurement cycle.

National government survey respondents were asked in what stages of the procurement cycle they are currently emphasising SPP/GPP, with results shown in Figure 18.

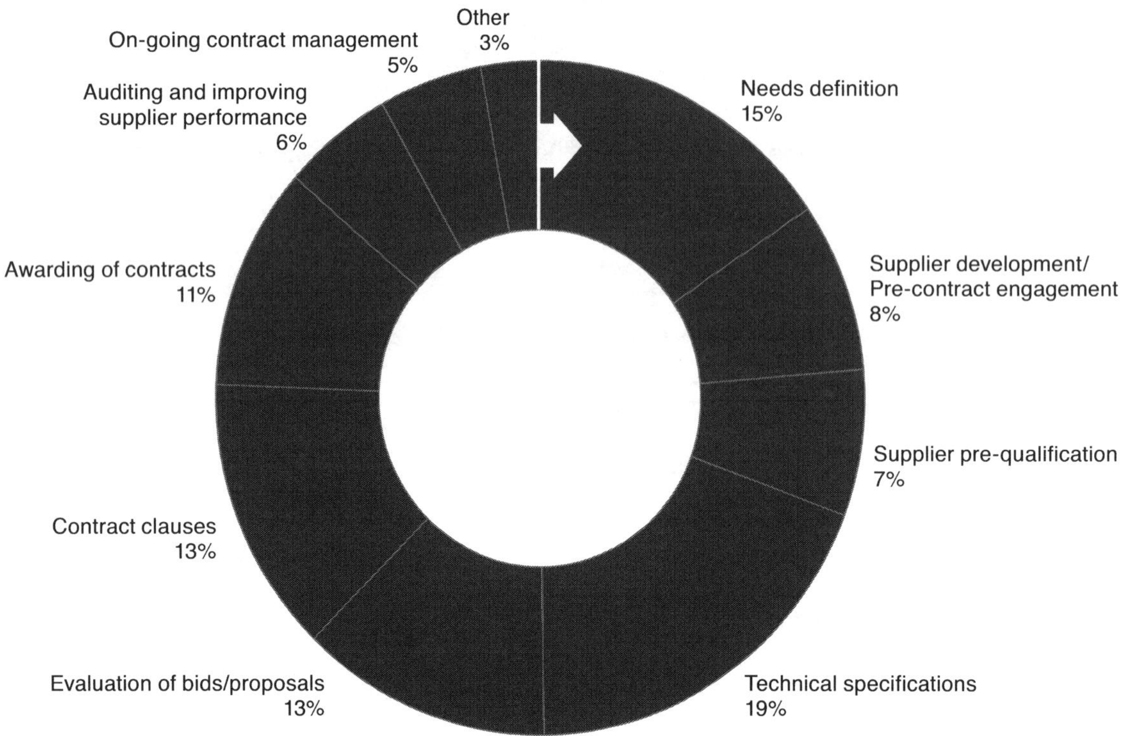

Figure 18: National government emphasis on SPP/GPP at different stages of the procurement cycle

Nearly 80 per cent of the respondents to this question chose more than one procurement cycle phase as currently being emphasized, providing some indication that national governments are taking a comprehensive approach. The results show that implementation is happening at nearly every stage of the procurement cycle, with the most emphasis being placed on "technical specifications", followed by "needs definition", then "contract clauses". Some respondents note that as with other questions, their answer would vary by both product category and also by agency or ministry. Others noted that they are seeking to "consume less" (which could be classified as part of a "needs definition" stage), and that implementation on SPP/GPP is currently somewhat ad-hoc.

In implementing any procurement, oftentimes agencies utilize a set of rules to guide final procurement decisions. National government survey respondents were asked to identify the "dominant awarding rule" used to determine contract awards by national procuring entities in their country, with results shown in Figure 19.

Price was considered the dominant awarding rule, followed by "value for money" which is a broader concept that allows for SPP/GPP criteria and oftentimes considers life cycle / whole of life costing. One respondent described the multi-step processes that procurers take to make decisions. It may include price considerations but also includes other aspects at other phases, such as quality, experience and responses to technical specifications.

To provide an external perspective on the issue, stakeholder survey respondents were asked their impression of how SPP/GPP criteria are typically weighted compared with other procurement criteria such as price, with results shown in Figure 20.

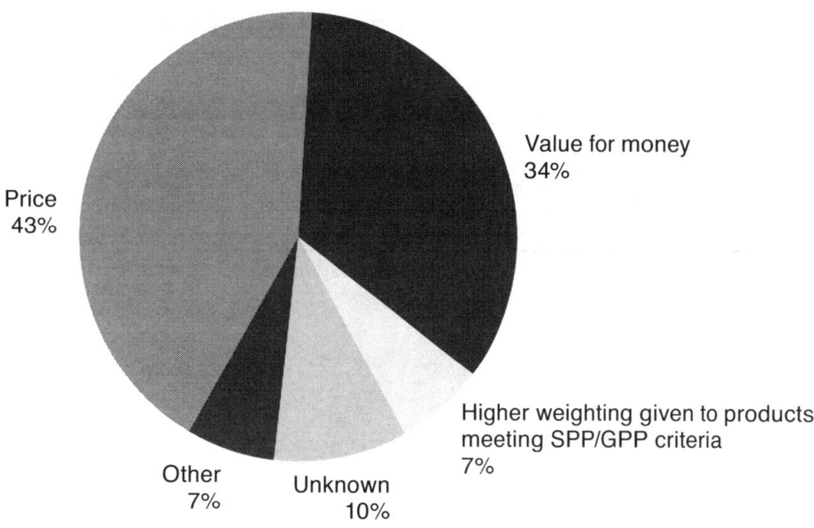

Figure 19: Dominant awarding rules by national governments for procurement

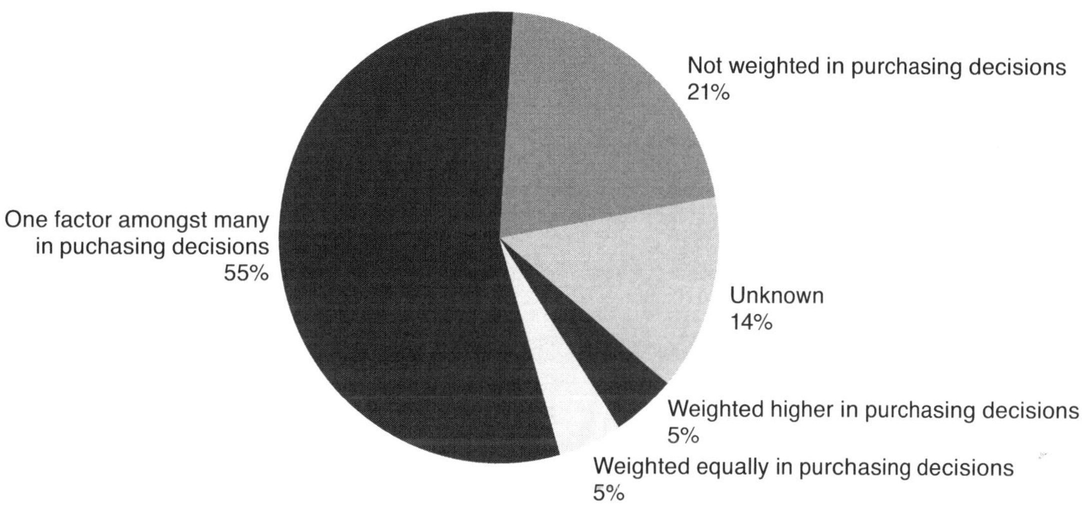

Figure 20: How national governments' weighting of SPP/GPP in decisions is perceived by stakeholders

For the most part, stakeholders have the impression that SPP/GPP criteria were weighted as one factor amongst many or simply not weighted, and thus not given any special priority in final purchase decisions. Only 5 per cent of respondents stated that SPP/GPP criteria are weighted higher than other procurement criteria. In some of the comments it was noted that the weighting of 10-20 per cent was given to the SPP/GPP criteria relative to other factors being considered. Another respondent commented that SPP/GPP criteria are being weighted "more highly as time goes on", or that SPP/GPP criteria are instead being used as minimum requirements. These findings indicate some stakeholder uncertainty around procurement practices having changed as a result of SPP/GPP policies.

3.3.4 The Use of Product Guidelines, Ecolabels and Life Cycle Costing

The development of product guidelines or criteria can be thought of as an indicator of implementation of SPP/GPP, as developing these tools can be a resource intensive process. In some countries newer to SPP/GPP, such as Romania, national guidance exists for a few product groups. For countries with a longer history of SPP/GPP work, the number of products categories with guidelines tends to be larger.

National government survey respondents were asked to identify the product categories that are covered by SPP/GPP guidelines in their country, and were provided a standard list of product categories (based on the European Commission's list of product categories and guidelines[58]). Results are shown in Figure 21.

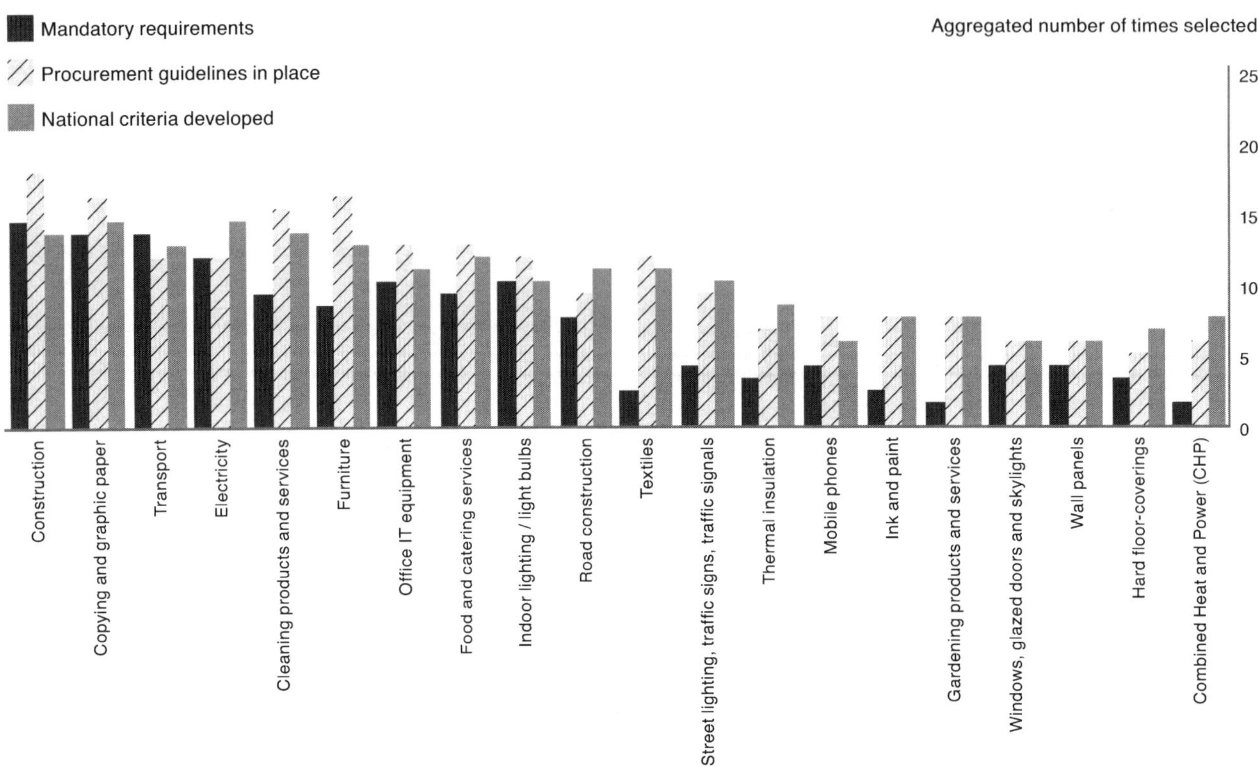

Figure 21: Product category guidelines with mandatory requirements, procurement requirements in place or national criteria developed (national government respondents)

The categories most often mentioned as having national criteria developed were construction, copying paper, cleaning products and transportation. Those with the most mandatory guidelines in place were nearly all energy-efficiency related: construction, transportation (largely vehicle fuel efficiency), electricity, office IT equipment and indoor lighting/light bulbs. The categories most often mentioned as having national criteria currently being developed were: construction, copying paper, cleaning products and transportation.

As previously mentioned, ecolabels and sustainability standards[59] are often used by procurers to identify products that meet SPP/GPP criteria, and also often inform product category guidelines. The national approach to ecolabels and voluntary standards systems is likely to influence the implementation approach taken to SPP/GPP. Some countries provide their purchasers guidance in how to use an array of different ecolabels and standards, while other countries align their national programmes on SPP/GPP on the criteria and work of national ecolabelling bodies. For example, Norway has a long tradition of emphasizing ecolabelling requirements on procured products, and the Japanese government supported ecolabel is highly favoured in GPP implementation.[60]

---

58   European Commission, 2012b.

59   Ecolabels are signs or logos indicating an environmentally preferable product, service or company, based on defined standards or criteria. Ecolabel Index, 2012.

60   CSCP and Wuppertal, 2007.

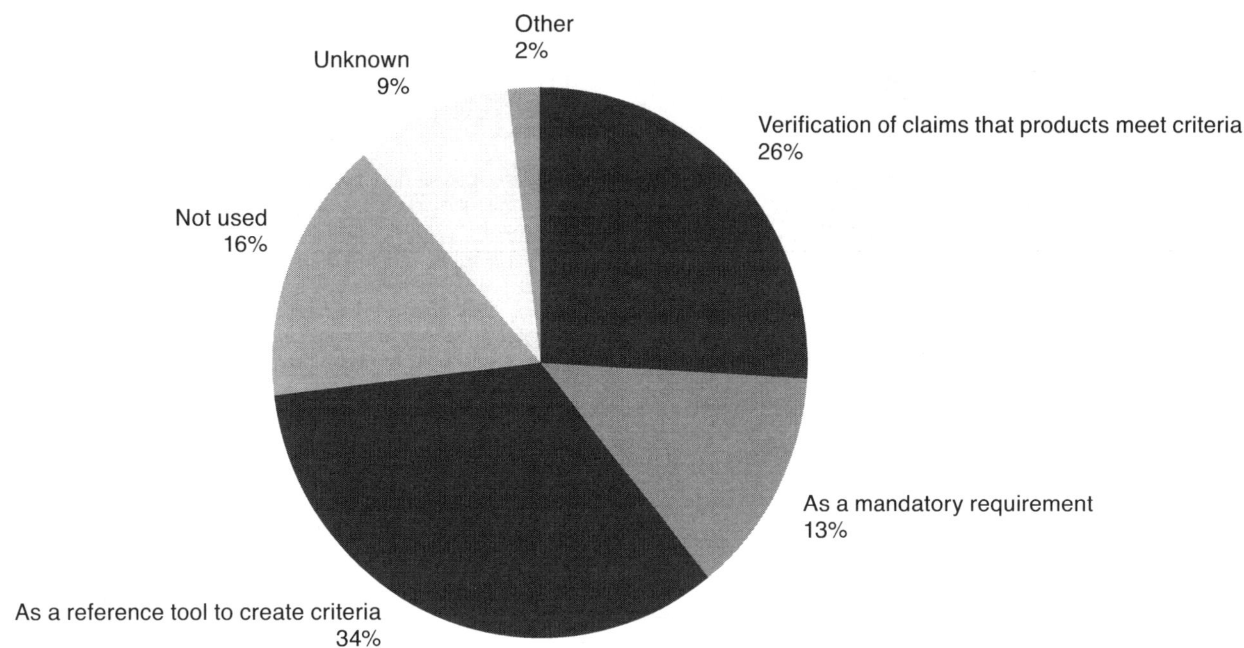

Figure 22: Different uses for ecolabels and voluntary standards in SPP/GPP

Survey respondents (both national government and stakeholders) were asked how are ecolabels and voluntary sustainability standards used today by national procurement entities, with results shown in Figure 22.

The most common use for ecolabels and voluntary sustainability standards were cited as a reference tool in creating criteria, and secondly for verification. Fewer stated that ecolabels are used as mandatory requirements, though one respondent noted that some government-operated ecolabels may be used in this way, while non-government operated ecolabels may not in their country. Interestingly, 16 per cent of respondents stated that ecolabels are "not used" in procurement.

Respondents also noted that the use of ecolabels can be limited, ad-hoc, varying by product category or contract, and sometimes is actually "erroneous" - contravening directives or even regulation. Another respondent noted that ecolabelled products are sometimes considered as priority in requirements, but are not mandatory.

In some regions, notably Europe, it is not possible to require conformance with particular ecolabels given possible trade implications.[61] In this case, product guidelines and criteria are issued instead, with the ecolabel being one (but not the only) way of demonstrating conformance to those criteria where relevant.

Another tool often linked to sustainability considerations in procurement is the use of Life Cycle Costing (also known as "whole of life costing"). Life cycle costing is a technique that helps purchasers consider all the costs that will be incurred during the lifetime of the product, work or service, including purchase price and associated costs (such as deliver, installation etc.), operating costs (including energy, spares, maintenance), and end of life costs such as decommissioning and disposal.[62]

National government survey respondents were asked the extent to which LCC is currently being used in their administration, with results shown in Figure 23.

---

61   European Commission, 2012c.
62   European Commission, 2004c.

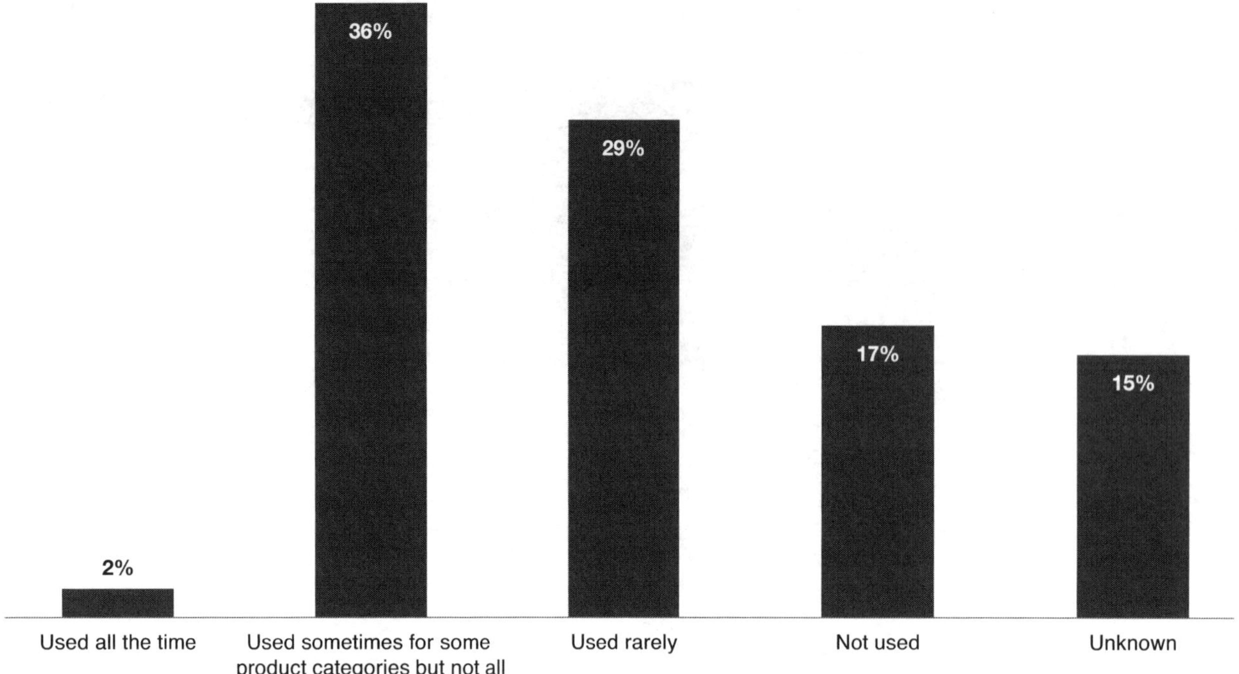

Figure 23: How well used is life cycle costing by national governments

The results indicate that for the majority of respondents, life cycle costing is being used "sometimes for some product categories", or that is being "used rarely". A total of 17 per cent of respondents state that it is not being used at all in their country. One respondent commented that they are in the process of using life cycle costing but that it is not yet fully implemented. Future research could investigate to which product categories life cycle costing is being applied, for example, with larger capital-intensive projects (where maintenance costs may be significant), or across all product categories. Niels Ramm from UNOPS remarked, "given recent economic conditions, we see more emphasis on life cycle costing. We also see more people asking fundamental questions about whether or not they really need to buy a product or service and if can they do without it. Simply not buying is sometimes (but not always) the greenest option."

There is also variation in how stringent or rigorous the SPP/GPP criteria are — whether criteria are developed by ecolabelling program as embedded in standard, or recognised in a published product category guideline. In the EU, the notion of "deep green" connotes green procurement that takes into account the full effects on the environment exerted by the product or service over its life-cycle from "cradle to grave" (as recommended in the OECD Council Recommendation on Improving the Environmental Performance of Public Procurement[63]). However, the ability to address and emphasize all of these environmental characteristics varies. In the EU, the award criteria have to be related to the subject matter of the contract, i.e. the product, and not to the supplier as such.[64] However, there are discussions underway about extending GPP requirements in the EU to include production methods. In Japan, both the environmental performance of the product as well as the supplier is considered.

---

63   OECD, 2007.
64   Michelsen & de Boer, 2009.

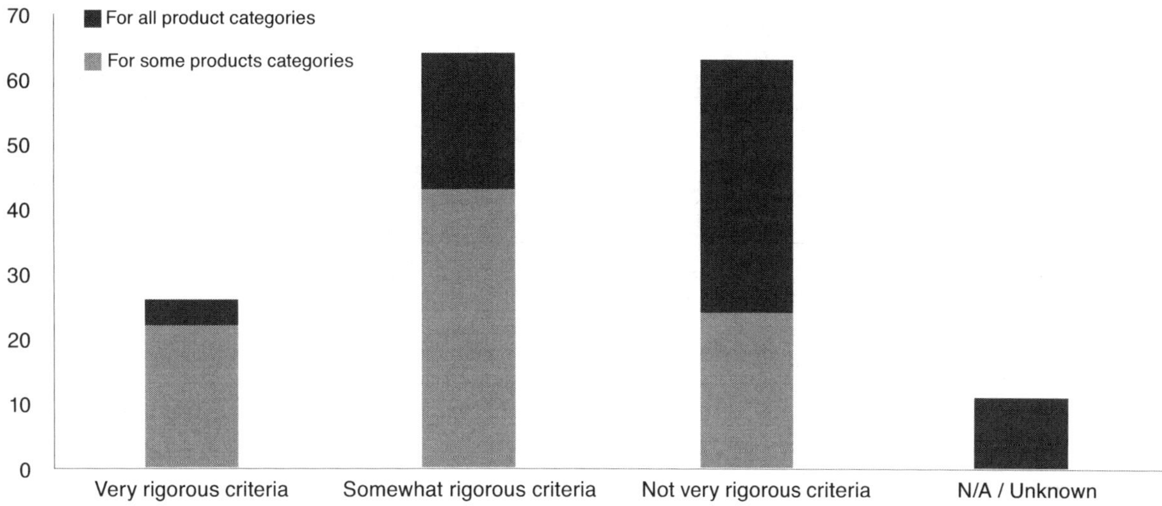

Figure 24: How stakeholders perceive the rigor of national governments' SPP/GPP criteria

Stakeholders survey respondents were asked as to their perceptions of the strength of the SPP/GPP criteria used by their national governments, with results shown in Figure 24.

Very few stakeholders believed that "very rigorous" criteria were being used across all product categories; although some respondents did think that for some product categories at least, there appeared to be rigorous criteria in use. The rest of the respondents thought that there were "somewhat rigorous" criteria being used in some product categories; or that not very rigorous criteria are being used across all product categories. These findings suggest that there is still some way to go before SPP/GPP by governments is both rigorously and consistently applied.

3.3.5 Discussion of Implementation

Although worldwide there is a plethora of policy and regulatory frameworks pertaining to SPP/GPP, policies and action plans do not always translate into clear changes in how procurement is implemented. Further, in practice, guidelines and criteria alone do not always manage to convince procurement professionals to follow up on their stated requests to suppliers. This disconnect is evidenced in the survey findings that show that despite having policies in place, tools such as life cycle costing are not being rigorously applied, and oftentimes the dominant awarding rule or decision-criteria still appears to come down to price.

A variety of approaches to SPP/GPP implementation found in the research speaks to a rather scattered approach. Countries appear to be pursuing several different SPP/GPP and SCP activities simultaneously, and that these activities can be mutually reinforcing, but they are not always very well coordinated.

Why do approaches vary so much, and which approaches tend to yield the best results? It has been argued that an important enabling condition influencing the means of implementation is the degree of centralization of procurement decisions.[65] A minimum of effective governance in the public sector is needed in order to implement SPP/GPP and good procurement principles such as competition, transparency, and fairness also need to be reflected in SPP/GPP.

The survey results revealed that there appears to be a gap between what national agencies are doing on SPP/GPP and what broader stakeholders think that they are doing. In such cases, stakeholders are either being more critical of activities, or are not well informed of the breadth of activity taking place. There is some scepticism about the level of stringency and rigor in criteria, and how sustainability factors are taken into account in final procurement decisions. There is now a wider acknowledgement of the need for GPP to become more comprehensive, i.e. "to go back all the way to the mine" as one survey respondent put it. The question is how to realistically do this work, given legal and technical constraints.

Miguel Porrúa of the Organization of American States (OAS) stated, "many governments think that SPP is costly, and this is a big obstacle. They would be willing to take more action if they also knew the cost of environmental issues left unchecked. We should also be asking: what is the cost of not doing SPP?" It is too early to judge whether the different implementation practices by national governments are in fact leading to improved environmental and/or social outcomes. How to assess progress and compare different implementation approaches is a key challenge for the SPP/GPP community.

---

65   OECD, 2003.

3.4 Monitoring, Reporting and Indicators of SPP/GPP

One of the current challenges facing SPP/GPP programmes is creating good monitoring, evaluation and reporting systems that track progress on implementation of SPP/GPP and communicate the environmental and social benefits being achieved.

Several factors contribute to the difficulty of creating reliable and comparable indicators for SPP/GPP, including:

- The lack of good infrastructure for collecting procurement data and difficulty in tracking procurement activity, given the sometimes complex and decentralised approaches to public procurement. Precise information on how much is actually purchased in different product categories can be difficult to obtain;

- Difficulties in precisely defining what counts as a sustainable or green procurement, product and/or service given the many and various ecolabels, standards and claims in circulation, and differences between "dark green" and "light green" (i.e. more or less rigorous) requirements; and

- The lack of a well established methodology for how to best monitor and evaluate the environmental and/ or social benefits being created by greener or more sustainable products, and even more difficulty in tracing those benefits back to purchasers' interventions.

Experience gained to date by countries show that certain institutional measures greatly enhance the ability to monitor and report on SPP/GPP implementation, namely:

- The use of e-procurement platforms;

- Having official targets and mandates that are reported against;

- The ability to collect data on SPP/GPP through indicators being integrated into standard procurement procedures as routine practice (as opposed to adding it later or having a separate system to track results);

- The use of clearly defined and agreed upon environmental and social criteria, facilitated, for example, by a list of pre-screened ecolabels and standards; and

- Making the link between SPP/GPP and financial measures and/or other policy goals (such as job creation). The ability to demonstrate the savings generated (if any) and green jobs created (if any) incentivizes the implementation of SPP/GPP as well as monitoring.

Government survey respondents were asked whether they were monitoring SPP/GPP currently, with results shown in Figure 25.

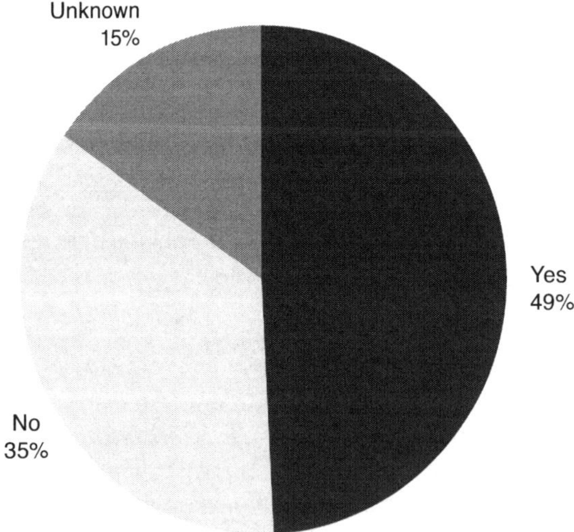

Figure 25: The existence of national government monitoring practices for SPP/GPP

Half of countries surveyed stated that some kind of monitoring and evaluation system for SPP/GPP is now in place, though it was noted that in some cases this monitoring is very limited. Many respondents (15 per cent) didn't know if SPP/GPP was being monitored or not, while others noted that a monitoring program is currently being devised.

For those that were monitoring SPP/GPP two measures were queried in the survey: the amounts spent on SPP/GPP goods and services, and/or the volumes or quantities of SPP/GPP goods and services, with results shown in Figure 26.

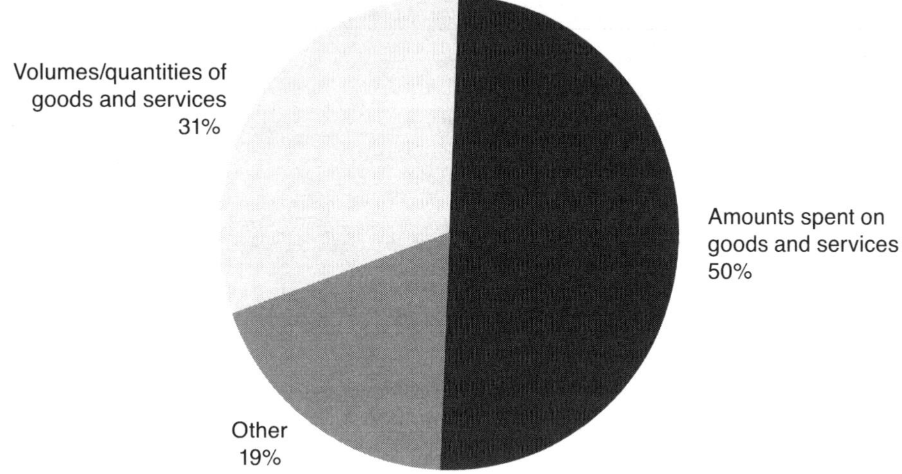

Figure 26: Measures by which national governments are monitoring SPP/GPP

Of those that had indicated a monitoring system for SPP/GPP being established, 67 per cent indicated that the primary measure of SPP/GPP activity is based on the amount being spent (e.g. in dollar terms). A total of 44 per cent stated that it is the volume or quantities of goods and services meeting SPP/GPP criteria that are monitored.

National government survey respondents were also asked whether any reporting on SPP/GPP is taking place in their country.

Significant numbers of countries in all regions are not currently reporting on SPP/GPP even if they are undertaking some form of internal monitoring. According to survey respondents, those that are producing reports are most often in Europe.

3.4.1 Indicators Currently Used to Track SPP/GPP

The following three types of indicators used to track SPP/GPP monitoring were found in reports and literature on SPP/GPP: those tracking policies, laws, and plans; those measuring implementation; and those measuring impact.[66] Examples within each category include:

a) Policies/Laws/Plans
- Incorporation of SPP/GPP into National Action Plans or other national objectives;
- Existence of SPP/GPP specific mandates and who must meet them;
- Existence of SPP/GPP targets or other commitments;
- Extent to which SPP/GPP requirements are mandatory or voluntary;
- Whether SPP/GPP is integrated into procurement regulations;
- Whether SPP/GPP is integrated into environmental regulations, policies; and
- Ministries engaged in the design and implementation of SPP/GPP policies

b) Implementation Activities
- SPP/GPP as a percentage of total public procurement (in terms of monetary value);
- SPP/GPP as a percentage of total public procurement (in terms of the number of contracts);
- The environmental impact of SPP/GPP in terms of CO_2 emissions/ resource efficiency;
- The financial impact of SPP/GPP in terms of the lifecycle costs

c) Impact Indicators
- The per cent environmental impact of SPP/GPP in terms of CO_2 emissions/ resource efficiency;
- The per cent financial impact of SPP/GPP in terms of the lifecycle costs; and
- The number of green products on the market before and after a given SPP/GPP policy is enacted, for example, as measured by the number of certified products in a given product category and/or market share.

All survey respondents were asked their opinions on a list of possible indicators for SPP/GPP and whether they thought the indicator was "useful and measurable", "useful but not measurable" or "not useful", with results shown in Figure 27.

There were some differences of opinion as to what is a useful versus actually measurable indicator for SPP/GPP. The indicator that had the greatest positive response was "The percentage of total national public procurement governed by SPP/GPP policy (measured by monetary value)". The next most popular indicator was "The percentage of contracts requiring that products meet certification requirements", though some still thought that this would be difficult to measure. Indicators dealing with environmental and social impacts were highlighted as the most difficult to measure, even if they would be considered useful. One respondent commented that not all green products are certified, a measure that required certification could potentially exclude many green products and services and therefore under-report.

Some of the comments shed light on the findings. One respondent stated that, "Although many of the indicators may be measurable, there may be challenges to measuring in our country"; and another respondent stated that "these are useful and measureable, however, access to data and data validation will be critical to the performance metrics."

National government survey respondents were asked to estimate the percentage of their country's spending governed by SPP/GPP in order to determine the feasibility of gathering this type of information. The question was posed for two reasons: to gather some initial data, and to test the viability of this type of indicator. Results are shown in Figure 28.

Even though an estimate was requested (so the response did not need to be based on actual data), a large portion of respondents either skipped the question, stated that it is not currently measured, or stated that the answer was unknown. For those that posited an estimate, the largest number of respondents selected that "less than five per cent" is currently governed by SPP/GPP policies.

Many comments were made to the effect that it is not possible to answer this question because data is not collected due to a lack of monitoring and reporting systems; and moreover, that the definition of GPP/SPP is still not clear enough to draw a clear line between what is SPP/GPP and what is not.

---

66   This builds on the European Commission's efforts to monitor GPP which established two types of indicators: quantitative indicators to assess the progress of the policy and its impact on the supply side, and impact-oriented indicators allowing assessment of the environmental and financial gains made. This monitoring methodology was tested in the 2009 study undertaken on behalf of the Commission, PriceWaterhouse Coopers (PwC), Significant, and Ecofys, 2009; and CEPS and The College of Europe, 2012.

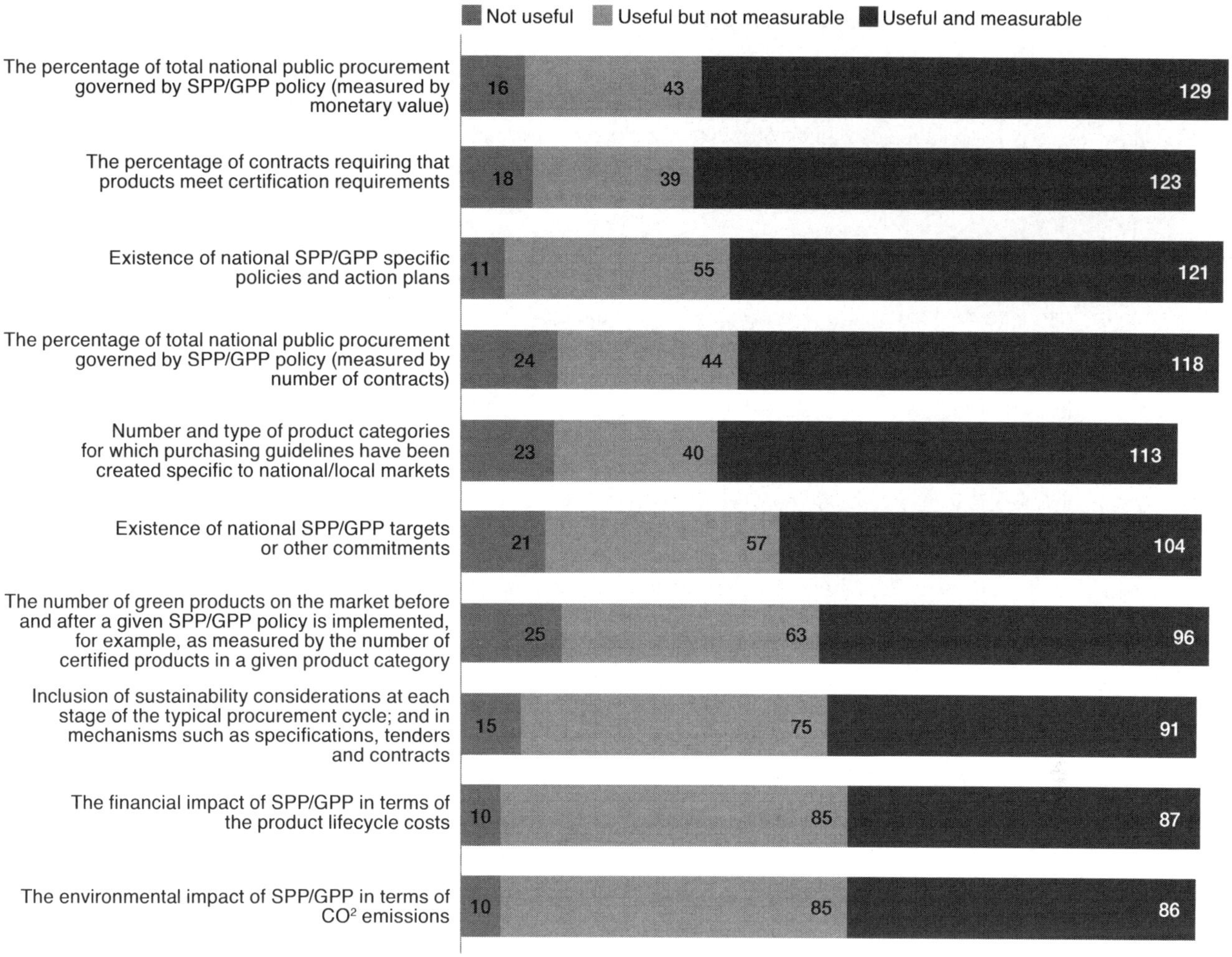

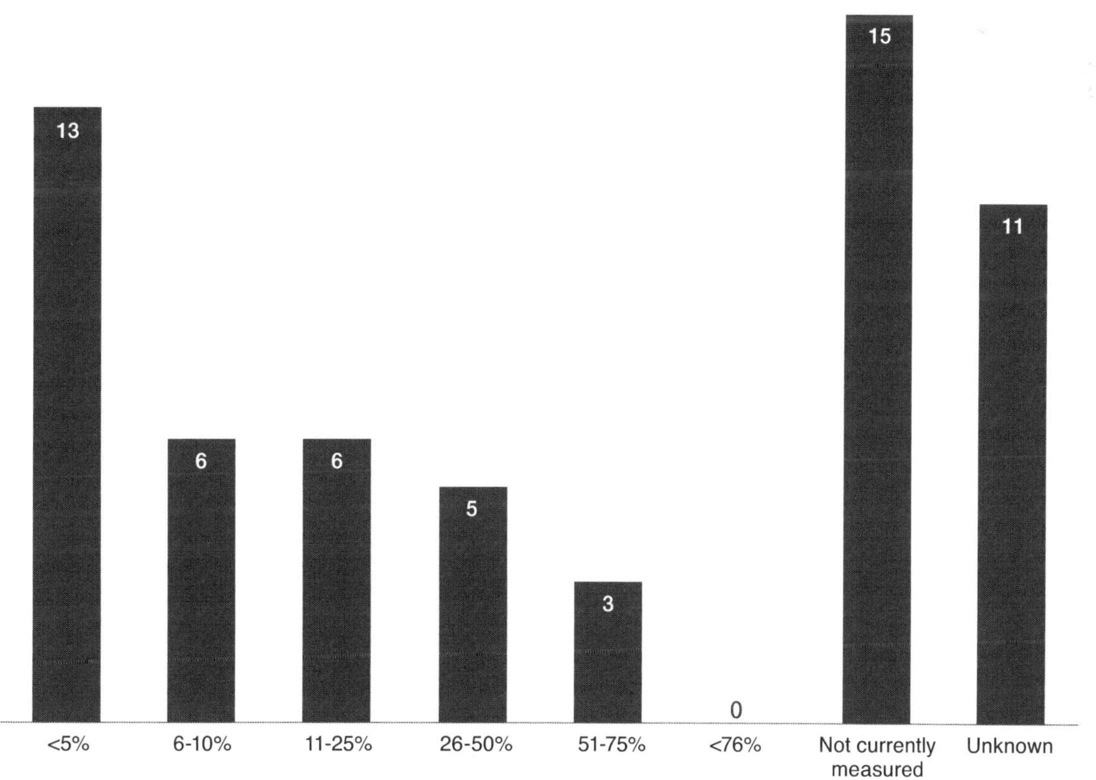

Figure 27: Support for different SPP/GPP indicators

Figure 28: Estimates by national governments on the percentage of their total spending governed by SPP/GPP policies/actions

3.4.2 Discussion of Indicators and Reporting Frameworks

Among the experts consulted for this report, the most commonly suggested indicator for SPP/GPP was whether tender documents included environmental/social criteria; and the survey results also supported this type of indicator as being useful. However, one interviewee cautioned that in measuring implementation, any data gathered on tender documents must be accompanied by an understanding of how weighting systems and/or final decisions are made. Even if there are environmental or social considerations in the tender document, the final decision may be made on price or other standard criteria.

Other studies reveal that the placement of sustainability criteria in calls for tenders does not necessarily mean that procurement agents have the insight and knowledge to use the information provided by suppliers. In a Norwegian study from 2009,[67] it was shown that suppliers' perception of the procurers' efforts suggests a much lower focus on environmental aspects than the municipalities had claimed. The study also showed that approximately half of the potential suppliers were "almost never" requested to provide information on the environmental impacts of their products and services or on their environmental management system. Interestingly, more than 75 per cent of the suppliers in that study perceived that environmental performance information "was of no real importance" in the final selection of suppliers, speaking to the importance of measuring action as well as policy.

Data availability and/or quality will also influence results. For example, the European Commission notes that measuring GPP would be a different exercise if there were a central database for all purchases being made. Today, few countries are collecting quantitative information on the number of contracts awarded that take into account SPP/GPP criteria.[68] Indeed, one indicator for progress on SPP/GPP may well be the extent to which indicators themselves are being used by a given country.

As the findings from the survey revealed, determining what is a "green" or "social" criterion is not always straightforward and there are shades of green — i.e. there are different degrees of rigor that can be applied. Some product categories may be more environmentally or socially impactful than others. Additional information is needed to truly understand what is being done, and how meaningful that activity is in actually addressing sustainability concerns.[69]

Clearly there is much work ahead in determining a common and measurable set of indicators for tracking progress on SPP/GPP implementation. Measurement approaches will also need to be suitable to the policy, implementation approach and hurdles in particular countries and regions, and to provide a well-rounded view. In general, the best practice recommendation is to create a set of indicators to measure SPP/GPP, and to select indicators for which there is a realistic chance of gathering reliable data. An international framework to monitor and evaluate SPP/GPP is needed to enable benchmarking, stimulate competition, and potentially improve the implementation of SPP/GPP.[70] The development of robust indicators will be the subject of future research and analysis undertaken in the framework of the SPPI.

---

67   Michelsen and Boer, 2009.

68   OECD, 2011.

69   OECD, 2007.

70   Benchmarking enables and motivates one to determine how well one's current practices compare to others practices, experience best practices in action, locate performance gaps prioritize opportunities and areas for improvement, and improve current levels to world class standards. A thorough discussion of environmental benchmarking can be found in e.g. Bolli and Emtairah, 2001.

3.5 Drivers and Barriers for SPP/GPP

There is significant activity on SPP/GPP occurring in many different countries around the world even if it is tricky to monitor and evaluate precisely. This section explores some of the drivers to that uptake and the current barriers to implementation being experienced. The enabling conditions for SPP/GPP in developing countries is then discussed.

3.5.1 Drivers for SPP/GPP

Survey respondents were asked to identify the top three factors that most drove the adoption of SPP/GPP in their country, with results shown in Figure 29.

The largest driver selected by respondents was national legislation, followed by strong political and organizational leadership and policy commitments. This suggests that for many countries, a top-down approach to policy and implementation provides the strongest driver. Other drivers mentioned by respondents beyond the options provided included: the use of mandates, voluntary consensus standards, dialogue with industry and the existence of a clear business case and financial return on investment (ROI) for SPP/GPP.

There were some notable differences between the drivers that national government respondents selected compared to the other stakeholder groups surveyed. In general, national government respondents placed more emphasis on capacity building, legislation, policy documents and political leadership than did other stakeholders, and placed less emphasis on leadership from the private sector and the effect of activist campaigns.

With respect to activist campaigns geared at addressing environmental/social priorities, it was noted that their impact varies somewhat by product category. For example, stakeholder and activist campaigns have driven the adoption of sustainable timber procurement policies. Others commented that in their country currently, there are not sufficiently strong drivers for SPP/GPP of any type listed here beyond international pressure. And finally one respondent commented that, "we have all the policies we need, now we (just) need to implement them".

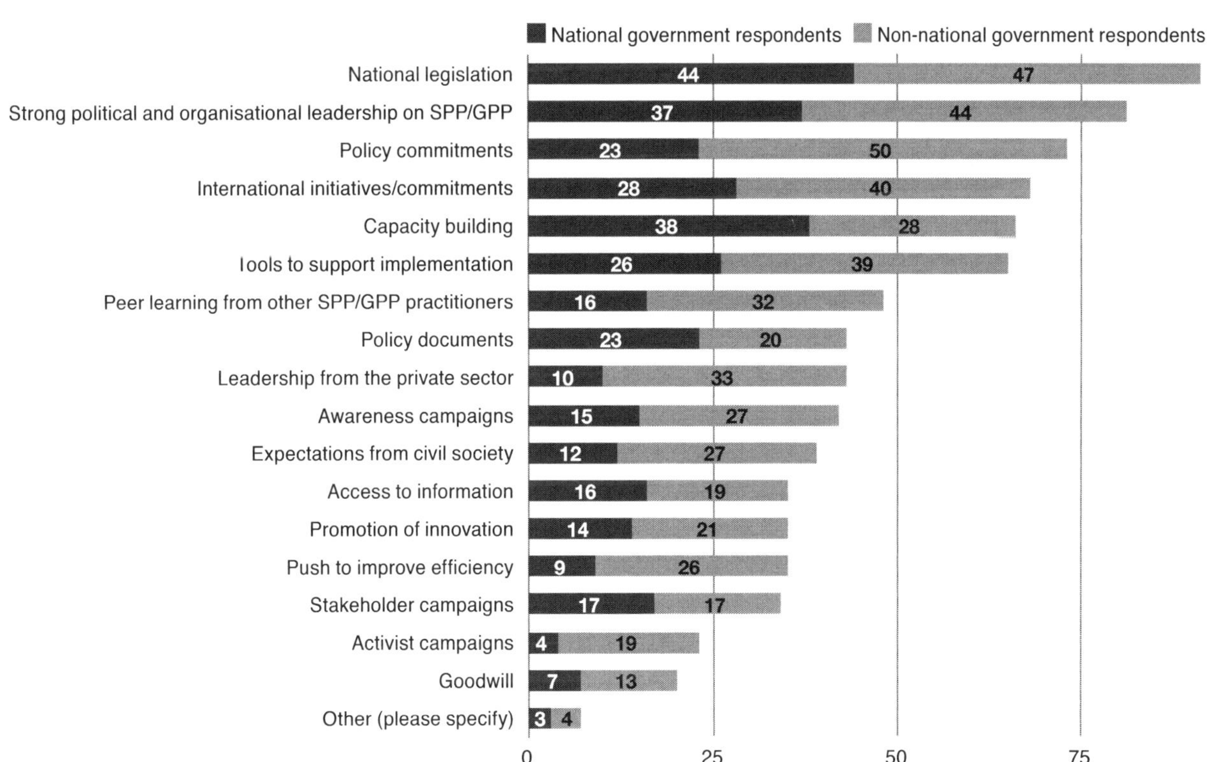

Figure 29: Drivers for SPP/GPP selected by all survey respondents

3.5.2 Barriers to SPP/GPP

Studies on SPP/GPP in recent years have highlighted the barriers and obstacles to adopting and implementing SPP/GPP with questions such as[71]:

- Why is implementation slow in some countries compared to others?
- What are the main difficulties that the procurement professionals face, and what resources do practitioners lack?
- What are the obstacles to a better dialogue between SPP/GPP policy and the market?

Barriers faced by national implementation authorities or procurement organizations relate to information, products, market actors and structures. However, it is difficult to generalise as to the relative importance of these barriers across different regions. Barriers tend to be context-dependent and are likely to vary with the stakeholder and region in question. To facilitate the implementation of SPP/GPP practices in their country, governments should focus on those barriers specific to their region and of concern to their stakeholders.

All respondents were surveyed as to their perception of barriers to SPP/GPP adoption in their country, with results shown in Figure 30.

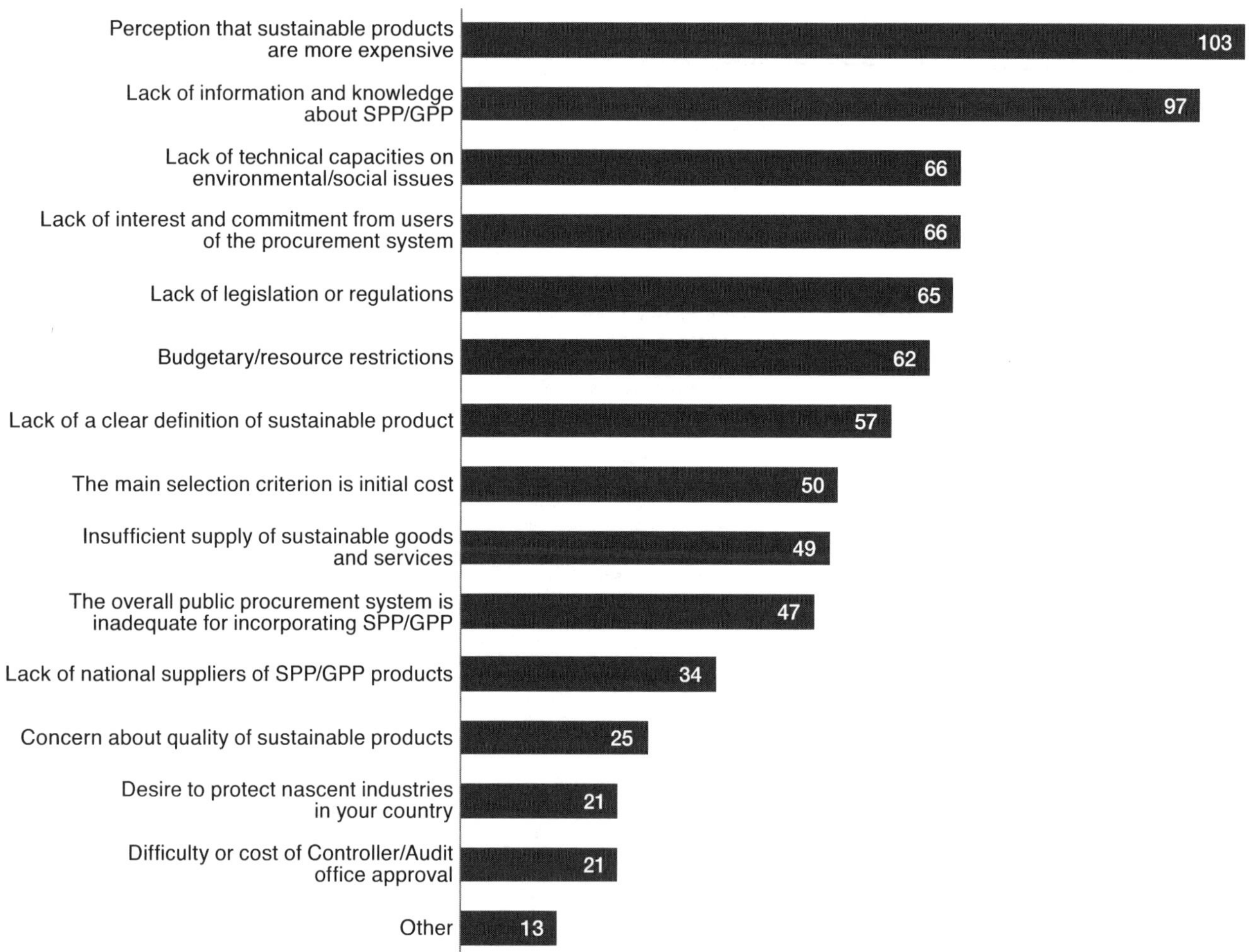

Figure 30: Barriers for SPP/GPP selected by all survey respondents

---

71   OECD, 2011 ; Bouwer et al., 2006; European Commission, 2012a; Sato, 2006.

As other studies on barriers to SPP/GPP have found, the perception that greener or more sustainable products are more expensive than conventional equivalents is common. However, it is unclear if this is actually the case, or just a perception of those surveyed. Other barriers cited included a lack of information and knowledge about SPP/GPP, and a lack of technical capacities on environmental and social issues.

National government representatives tended to rate higher the degree to which an insufficient supply of sustainable goods and services is a significant barrier than did other stakeholders. Several other barriers mentioned in comments beyond those listed as options, included:

- Lack of cooperation and integration of policy fields between government agencies;
- Uncertainty around verification of sustainability claims of products; scepticism about certain sustainability claims - is it really green?;
- Lack of consistent SPP/GPP standards across a variety of product categories;
- Political controversy over timber, chemicals and building standards stalling implementation in other categories;
- Lack of political will to invest the resources necessary to implement SPP/GPP;
- A lack of leadership on SPP/GPP from boards, senior managers and policy makers; and
- Civil servants having many other tasks and priorities beyond SPP/GPP.

The following sections discuss economic, policy and market related barriers in more depth.

3.5.2.1 Economy-Related Barriers

Recent economic conditions worldwide may be expected to affect the level and type of SPP/GPP activity being implemented. All survey respondents were asked how the current economic downturn affected the level of SPP/GPP activities by national governments, with results shown in Figure 31.

For 37 per cent of respondents, the current economic downturn has had no significant impact on the level of SPP/GPP being undertaken by national governments. However, some respondents noted that the commitment to SPP/GPP in their country was never very high to begin with, so the effect has been minimal. Five respondents (2 per cent) stated that it has actually led to an increased activity, with comments justifying this selection centering on some of the economic cost savings that are achieved through some SPP/GPP requirements, such as energy efficiency. A total of 29 per cent of respondents stated that the economic downturn has either "somewhat" or "significantly" stalled activity on SPP/GPP in their country.

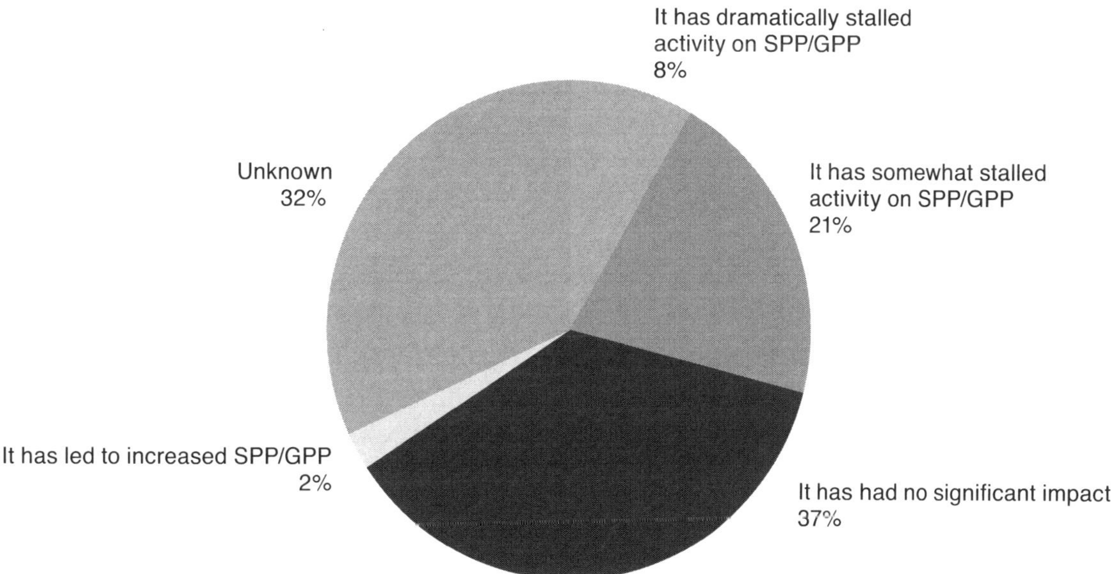

Figure 31: Views on how the economic downturn has affected SPP/GPP by survey respondents

3.5.2.2 Policy-Related Barriers

For countries just starting work on SPP/GPP, there is often a need to help social and environmental issues gain political support. The link between environmental and social issues and other political or economic priorities needs to be made explicit.

As discussed earlier, despite targets and mandates (e.g. in the UK, Denmark and Japan) implementation often remains uneven. Having specific laws and policies that promote, permit or require are necessary but not sufficient for SPP/GPP. Regions with multiple levels of procurement governance risk having differences in policy between different levels of government (national, sub-national), sending a confusing message to procurement organizations and suppliers, hindering effective implementation.[72]

In this context, a common barrier remains the anxiety and lack of clarity about what SPP/GPP practices are legally correct. This extends to concerns that SPP/GPP may be conceived as a trade barrier, contradicting international trade agreements and rulings.[73] Within the EU, the heterogeneity of the 27 Member States and the different national legislations regarding public procurement is problematic.[74] Said one interviewee, "the current political commitment in the EU is not enough to support GPP. The upcoming modernization of public procurement needs to focus on more clearly describing what is GPP and how it can be done".

3.5.2.3 Procurement-Related Barriers

If regulatory and policy requirements are not clear, many procurement officers will refrain from including considerations outside their usual norms and procedures.

It has been widely recognized that procurement organizations do not have the capacity or resources to also become environmental experts. A significant barrier for carrying out SPP/GPP in practice is the collection and evaluation of environmental information on products and services, as well as verifying claims from suppliers. To combat this, ecolabelled products have been promoted as helpful in the setting of technical specifications and providing independent verification.[75]

Without trusted information on which products are green, it can be difficult for procurement organizations to know if the market can offer products that meet expected ecolabels and standards. However with so many ecolabels and voluntary environmental standards now in existence (at least 432 ecolabels globally according to Ecolabel Index[76]), there is a need to differentiate between them. Some government agencies are creating criteria for determining which can be relied upon for government procurers in various product categories, such as in the US.[77]

Some argue that the more extensively SPP/GPP is implemented, the greater the challenges for procurement staff, so information or ecolabels alone will not solve the problem. In some places, social and ethical criteria reach beyond these standards, leading to a greater burden on the procurement organizations to have knowledge in new areas and evaluate different verification systems in order to make an assessment. As some countries such as the Netherlands move towards performance-based contracts designed to stimulate innovative responses, integrating sustainability dimensions can be complex. Even with sustainability-performance criteria as part of the contracts, understanding and rating the responses requires specialist sustainability expertise.

The range of formats and standards of environmental product information demands a broad set of competence and environmental expertise to evaluate. As a case in point, the European paper and pulp industry replaced ecolabelling with environmental product declarations (Paper Profile declarations[78]) creating challenges among buyers who struggled to know whether a particular product met a certain level of performance and whether that performance was "good enough" to be considered green.

---

72 Beláustegui, 2011.
73 Oshani et al., 2007.
74 CSCP and Wuppertal Institute, 2007.
75 Leire et al., 2012.
76 EcolabelIndex.com, 2012.
77 See the USA Case Study Appendix 1, and http://www.fedcenter.gov/Articles/index.cfm?id=17374
78 For example, see http://www.paperprofile.com/

Given tight budget constraints faced by most public sector organizations, perceptions regarding the financial viability and cost-effectiveness of SPP/GPP are critical.[79] The survey findings indicate that the perception of cost-effectiveness is a crucial barrier and common to all countries. For example, in Latin and Caribbean countries, government's impression of added cost from SPP/GPP has been seen as the largest obstacle, i.e. government would be willing to take SPP/GPP action if they could appreciate the financial risks and potential savings of considering environmental and social issues. Similarly, in the UK, the perception on the costliness of SPP/GPP among the procurement organizations is still considered a key barrier.

Variations in procurement agents' capacity to implement SPP/GPP is often linked with the type of product being procured. Similarly, the perception of costs of SPP/GPP also differs with the type of product being procured. It has been argued that procuring entities are more likely to pursue SPP/GPP in contexts where they perceive win-win situations and that they are more reluctant where the payoffs are unclear.[80] Also, different products bring different challenges to handle the environmental criteria and information generated. One such challenging area is chemical substances in products. Said one interviewee, "it is difficult because buyers don't buy the substances but rather the component that contain the substances". For products such as mass-produced cables and components, the high speed of the contracting process and of the structure of the spot/auction market results in a low degree of control in the supply chain.

An interesting policy response comes from Iceland, which is considering using economic instruments to stimulate greater SPP/GPP. The Icelandic 'Committee on the Promotion of Green Economy' has recently proposed a dedicated budget to support repaying public agencies for up to 20 per cent of the cost of goods and services that meet ISO Type I ecolabels' requirements.[81]

Others claim that efforts to encourage organizations to pay extra to address environmental risks are likely to be fruitless. Explained one interviewee, "it is evident that we need to expand the concept of 'best-value-for-money', already widely used in procurement systems, and integrate in the value part the full range of costs and benefits — economic, environmental and social".

3.5.2.4 Market-Related Barriers

The supply of green products and services can be a barrier to SPP/GPP — either because there is not enough to service the demand, or that supply is considered unreliable. For example, a negative trend in the uptake of SPP/GPP in 2005 was attributed to, among other things, the lack of access to green products in smaller communities and rural areas in some regions.[82] Many national governments have preference for the purchase of goods made in their country, so that international markets are unable to easily fill in any gaps.

The UNEP SPP Guidelines[83] recommend countries undertake a "Market Readiness Analysis" study relatively early in their design of a SPP/GPP plan to understand the likely impact of a given SPP/GPP action on the market, and to address questions of quantity and reliability of supply. Several interviewees likewise recommended that countries conduct market engagement strategies (within the constraints of their rules for good procurement practices) in order to prepare the market for forthcoming requirements and to give suppliers time to make any production changes needed.

Access to credible market data remains a barrier. A study in the EU found that the size of the market and variety of eco-friendly products available in different countries make it difficult to set common guidelines for products and to find quality market data to assess.[84]

---

79 Brammer & Walker 2010; Min and Galle, 2001.
80 Rao and Holt, 2005.
81 Icelandic National Parliament, 2001.
82 CSCP and Wuppertal Institute, 2007.
83 UNEP, 2012.
84 CSCP and Wuppertal Institute, 2007.

3.5.3 Enabling Conditions for Lesser Developed Countries

Developing and lesser-developed countries face some specific drivers and barriers to implementing SPP/GPP compared to more developed countries. Stakeholder survey respondents were asked to identify the most important "enabling conditions" (that is either drivers and/or barriers) specific to developing countries for SPP/GPP, with results shown in Figure 32.

The top enablers for SPP/GPP in lesser-developed countries were cited as political willingness and leadership, the same as the driver selected as highest priority for all countries. The next most important enabling condition cited was to "build capacity"; followed by having an "adequate legal framework". Other suggestions provided included: awareness raising workshops, technical capacity building, providing economic incentives, and gaining experience from developed countries.

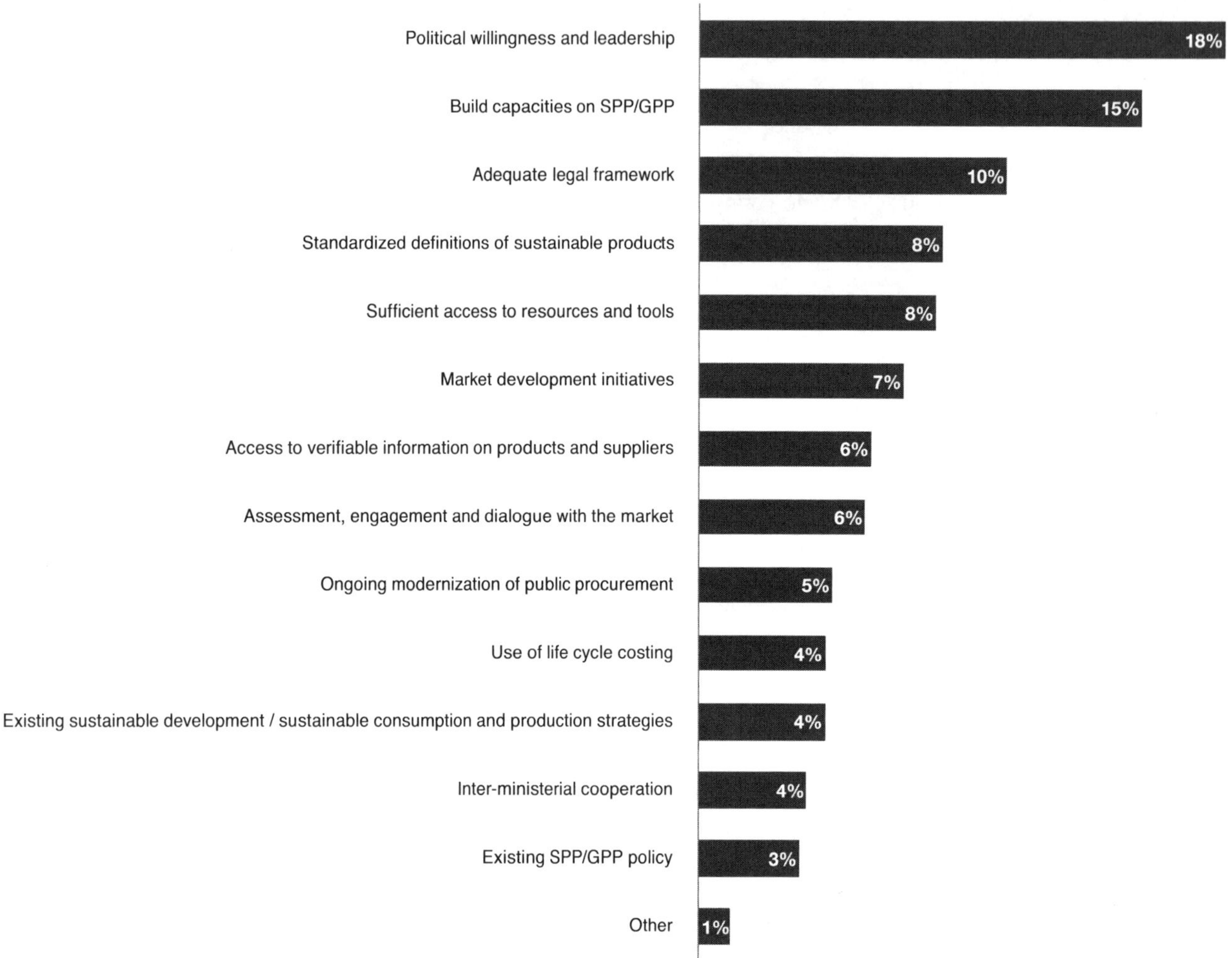

Figure 32: Enabling conditions on SPP/GPP in developing countries selected by survey respondents

Developing countries are at the moment struggling with some specific barriers:

First, the immediate undertaking of SPP/GPP implementation can be subordinate to other priorities that are needed for the immediate well-being of citizens.

Second, whereas developed countries have qualified human resources and funding, developing countries oftentimes lack both. They also often lack a modern procurement infrastructure or law, making it harder to introduce new requirements such as sustainability.

Third, expectations for the supply of sustainable products and services in developing countries need to be realistic. Technology is sometimes lacking to produce, standardise and market more sustainable products in many categories. In this light, however, it has also been stated that the industry and business in developing countries stand before a wave of opportunities to produce greener products both for domestic but also international markets.

3.5.4 Discussion of Drivers, Barriers and Enabling Condition

Overcoming barriers in SPP/GPP can be achieved not only by establishing a SPP/GPP policy, but also by changing of values and perceptions amongst all stakeholders towards its economic viability. Here the long-term effects of complementary SCP policy instruments such as ecolabels, standards and other tools promoting product-sustainability are important. Mechanisms and incentives are needed to encourage procurement officers to take on the challenge of implementing sustainability requirements.

Barriers may be more perceived than real. Even so, perceptions matter a great deal. The perception that the supply of green products and services are expensive, un-scalable and unreliable is still in wide circulation. One interviewee summed up the implication of this as, "the public procurement functions claim that the market can't supply them with the more sustainable products, but the suppliers of those products say that they can't get into public procurement".

While many of the drivers and barriers appear to be similar across regions, the enabling conditions needed to implement SPP/GPP in developing countries are more acute. Whereas governments in the more environmentally engaged countries struggle with barriers such as increasing the inclusion of a wider range of aspects, linking databases, creating training programs and synchronising ecolabel information[85], governments in developing countries are struggling to build more capacity in procurement in general, to build the case for starting work on SPP/GPP, and to link it to economic and political priorities.

---

85   CSCP and Wuppertal Institute, 2007.

3.6 Improving SPP/GPP Adoption and Implementation

The drivers and barriers articulated in the previous section suggest specific actions, for example, the lack of knowledge and capacity of procurement officers to successfully implement SPP suggests the need for training and capacity building. This section explores the activities most needed today at the national and international level, and also provides some perspective on forecast growth for SPP/GPP and what future research on SPP/GPP may be useful.

3.6.1 Country-Specific Needs

All survey respondents were asked what aspects of SPP/GPP needed the most work in their country, with results shown in Figure 33.

Of the list provided, training and engagement with suppliers rose to the top, followed by measurement of SPP/GPP activities and life cycle costing. The other need identified included the implementation of existing policies, increasing awareness in general, capacity building and training, development of implementation tools, measurement and reporting. Also mentioned was the need to develop product guidelines and criteria, better regulations, and greater certainty over the legal aspects of SPP/GPP.

Experts in the field of SPP suggest that any one of these actions alone is likely to not be enough. For example, an SPP expert observed, "you can't just rely on goodwill to do this work if you want it to become mainstream. You have to motivate people with day-to-day incentives, with personal development plans and recognition". Another invitee also noted that, "any training provided should be accompanied by on-going peer-to-peer learning and support. It needs to match the idiosyncratic and changing requirements they are facing, and the changing nature of what is designated as green or eco-friendly".

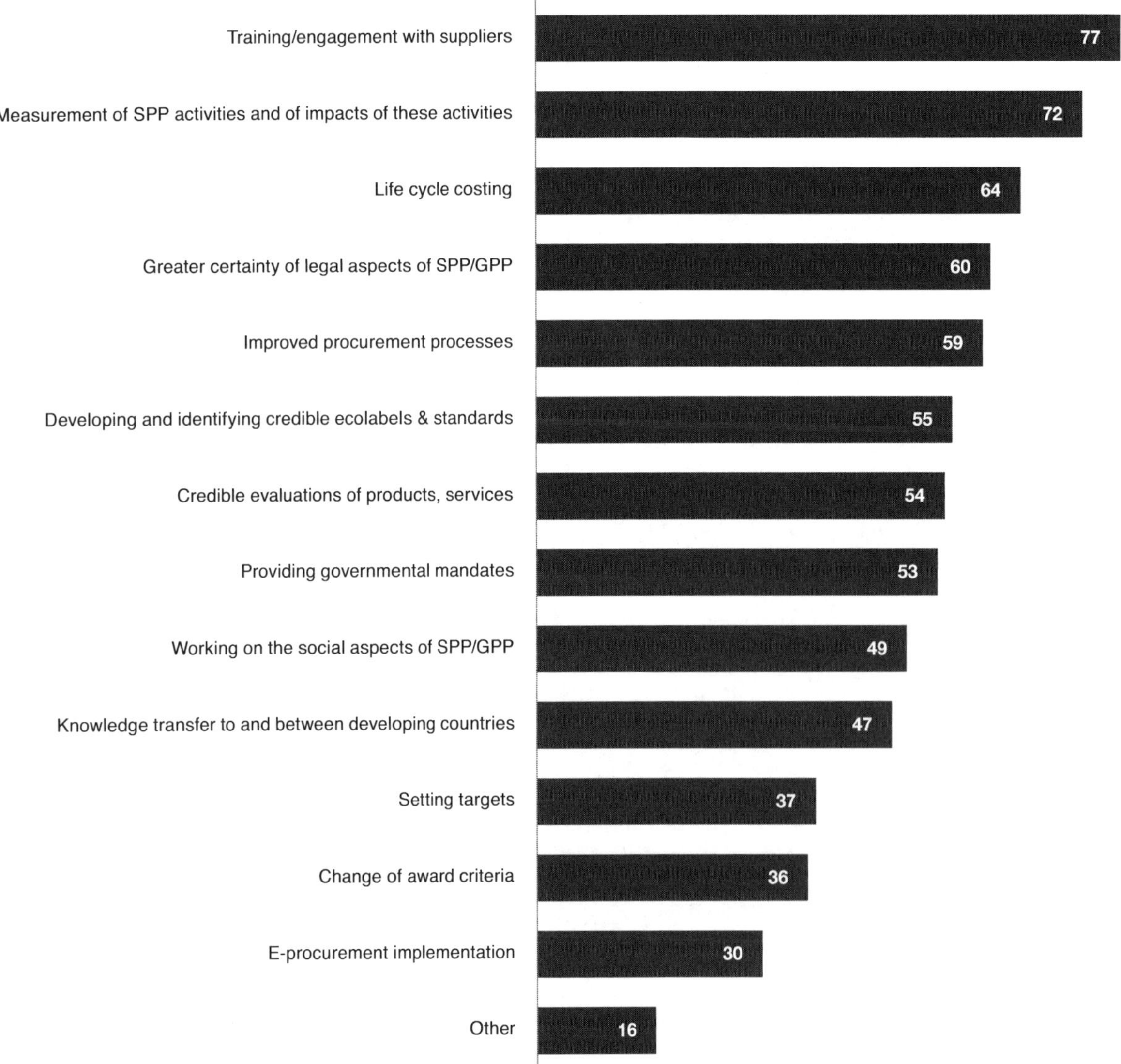

Figure 33: Activities "most needed" to grow SPP/GPP selected by survey respondents

A survey respondent reiterated taking a holistic approach to SPP implementation and focused on the need for improved monitoring and evaluation, "Even in advanced countries like Sweden, there is no follow up if a) products are only purchased from contracted suppliers and b) delivered products meet the environmental requirements of the purchase specification".

3.6.2 Need for International Collaboration

International initiatives on SPP/GPP, such as the SPPI, can help to guide and promote the adoption of SPP/GPP as well as bring a more coordinated approach to the topic. Akira Kataoka of the IGPN made the case for international harmonization when he stated that, "we already have a lot of information — in Japan alone there is GPP criteria in the law, GPN guidelines, ecolabel criteria, the products database. Instead we need to better harmonise the information and tools, both nationally and internationally."

All survey respondents were asked what the most useful or priority functions would be for an international initiative on SPP/GPP, with results shown in Figure 34.

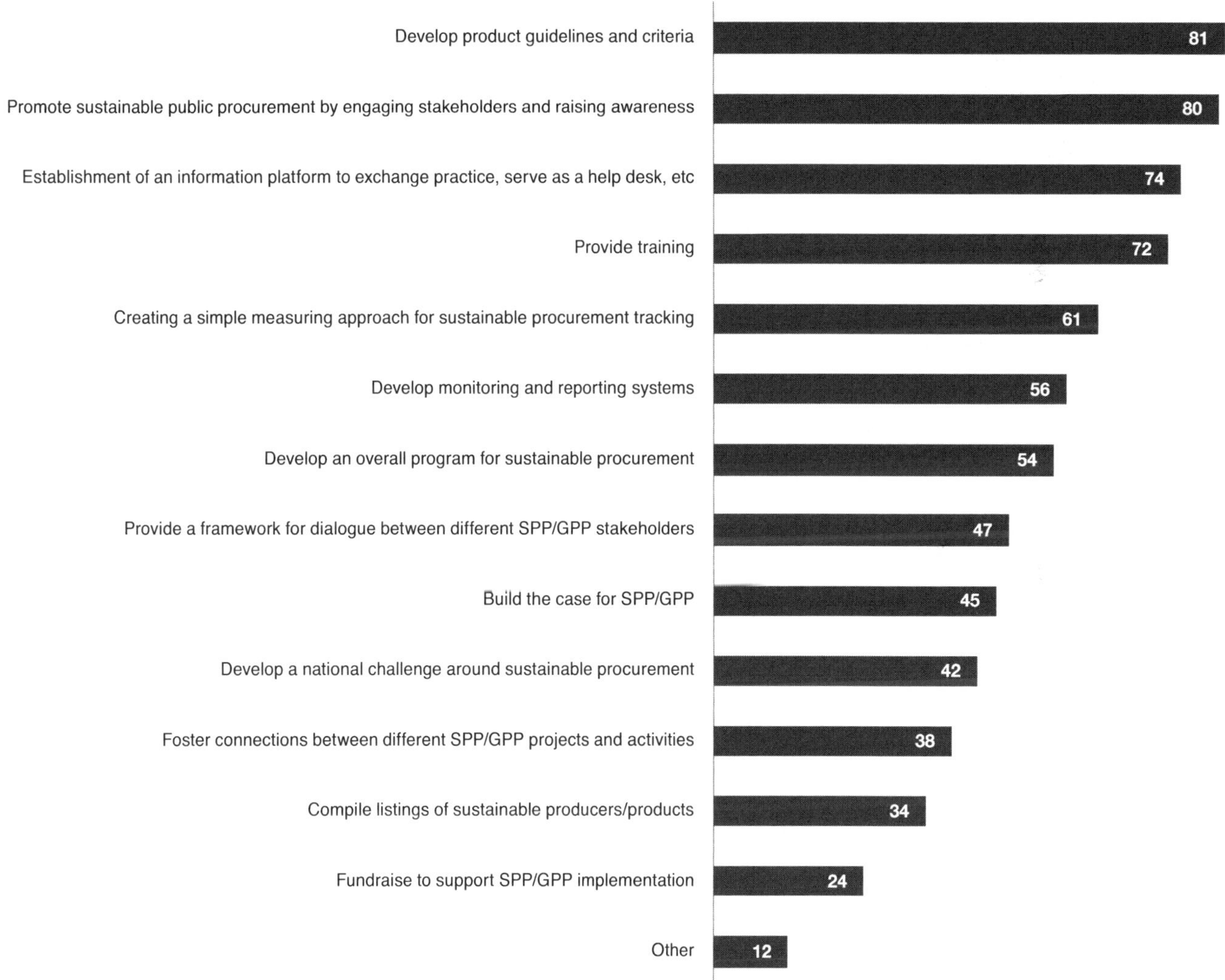

Figure 34: Priorities for an international initiative on SPP/GPP as selected by survey respondents

Speaking to the need for coordination and capacity building, the option selected most often was to "develop product guidelines and criteria"; followed closely by "promoting SPP/GPP" and "raising awareness to stakeholders". In addition, providing information platforms, training, and measurement and reporting systems were all considered useful functions of an international initiative. These results highlight the importance of coordination, capacity-building and information sharing. Respondents also recommended to: extend outreach to enterprise software providers, promote credible certifications for the verification of green claims, and facilitate the exchange of best practices between procurers.

Coordination is also needed with industry. As Sanjay Kumar from the Indian Railways put it, "GPP can not happen in vacuum, we need vendors to be on same page in the change-process". Another interviewee expanded on this point further, stating, "there is little point in throwing higher performance standards out there to meet if no companies can currently meet them. You need to give some advanced warning and even provide assistance to suppliers to meet the standards." Niels Ramm of UNOPS stated, "it is especially important that SMEs are able to participate in meeting SPP/GPP-led markets, and in some cases, they will need support to do so".

3.6.3 Forecast for SPP/GPP

For the next five years, SPP/GPP can be expected to continue to grow given current government commitments. To validate this expectation, all survey participants were asked to characterise their expectations for the growth of SPP/GPP activities in their country, with results shown in Figure 35.

A total of 49 per cent of respondents believe that over the next five years there will be some more SPP/GPP done by their national governments, and 35 per cent of respondents forecast that there will be "substantially more" SPP/GPP. A total of 14 per cent thought that it will remain "at about the same levels" and only 2 per cent thought that there will be "less than" or "dramatically less than" today. Several respondents commented that further work on SPP/GPP will be contingent on forthcoming elections in their country, pointing again to the importance of political drivers for SPP/GPP growth.

We should remember that respondents answering this question come from countries at very different stages of working on SPP/GPP. Some have been active in working on SPP/GPP for 10 or 15 years so any further work on SPP/GPP will be incremental, while others are only just starting, so may consider any forthcoming work on SPP/GPP "substantially more than today". Nonetheless, the expected trend is towards growth in SPP/GPP activity by national governments, with a good portion of respondents expecting substantial work on the topic to come.

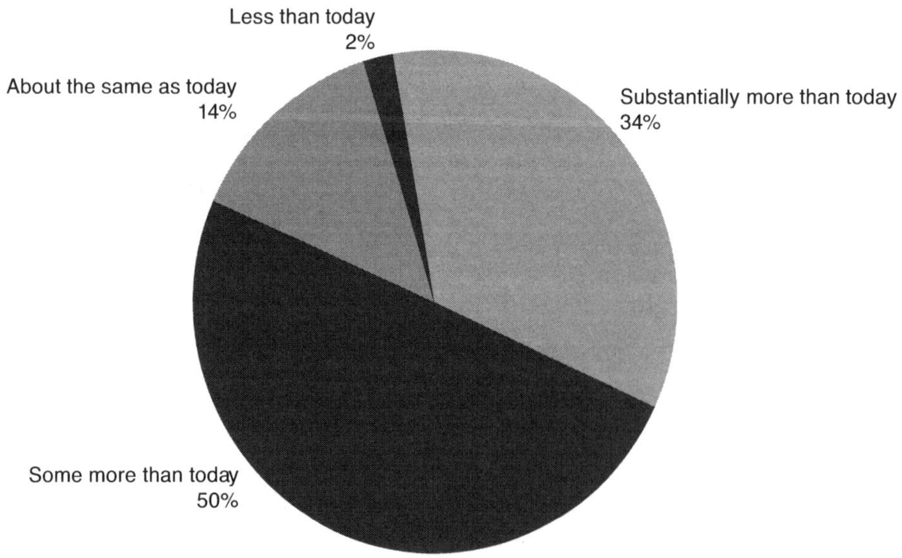

Figure 35: Forecast of survey respondents on the outlook for SPP/GPP

3.6.4 Other SPP/GPP Themes for Exploration

In order to gain a wider view of aspects of SPP/GPP not otherwise covered in this report, the final question of the survey asked all respondents whether there were additional topics on SPP/GPP not otherwise covered in the survey. The answers provide direction for future research on the State of SPP/GPP. Suggestions included:

- Investigating the benefits of SPP/GPP, for example, as a contributor to the green economy and job creation, as a stimulus for innovations and as an opportunity to revitalize and motivate procurement functions. For example, Pablo Prüssing Fuchslocher from Dirección ChileCompra stated, "done right, SPP can help to facilitate a new industrial revolution by introducing cleaner production, pollution prevention processes and cleaner technologies."

- Review the sustainable procurement activities of other stakeholders beyond national governments, from local and state government agencies, to private sector actors such as retailers and producers — both large and small;

- Investigate how national SPP/GPP policy intersects with international trade policies and WTO rules;

- Undertake further research and analysis of the legal aspects of SPP/GPP, including dedicated work on international trade, which can be perceived as a barrier to greater national government action;

- Better understand the influence of political parties and elections on SPP/GPP, and the degree to which political agendas may drive, overshadow or even impede implementation;

- Those operating within national government agencies mentioned the need for greater internal coordination of government agencies and the need to improve interagency cooperation in order to successfully implement SPP/GPP;

- Come to consensus on definitions of sustainable goods and services, with a greater focus on the selection and influence of tools such as ecolabels, standards and LCA

- Develop an informed view on how to best prioritise SPP/GPP efforts towards those goods and services purchased having the greatest environmental and social impacts;

- Focus on implementation with valuable lessons to be gained from "learning by doing".

The research conducted for this review revealed areas where the measurement, monitoring and reporting on SPP/GPP can be improved. Reporting on the state of SPP/GPP worldwide will benefit from a common indicator framework and comprehensive country-level reporting. Extending the research with different languages will also help to expand our understanding of SPP/GPP and the different approaches being taken.

4. Conclusions

This report on the global state of sustainable / green public procurement offered insight into the current state of play on national SPP/GPP efforts around the world, identified some particular needs and hurdles to be overcome, and indicated some potential pathways forward. It is clear that in the last five years, despite a major economic crisis and despite a changing political climate, the interest in SPP/GPP by governments and stakeholders is growing and has proven to be resilient.

In the period of analysis, many of the known leaders in SPP/GPP have deepened their commitment to implementation, extended the scope of product categories covered, and increased the number of environmental and social attributes being considered. Other countries newer to SPP/GPP are benefitting from this experience and from the general willingness of countries and SPP/GPP-promoting organizations to coordinate their work and share their findings. Many of the international, regional and national networks that aim to promote and support SPP/GPP are now working together so that there is a more unified, and hopefully less confusing, approach to what is a complex undertaking.

Financial and human resources are needed to support SPP/GPP activities across all countries — even those more experienced on the topic. Implementation of SPP policy is greatly accelerated with a dedicated budget. International initiatives can be effective in attracting the necessary resources and helping to develop communities of practice to enable peer-to-peer learning.

In taking a global approach to studying the state of play in SPP/GPP, much variation in terms of the "who, what, where, how" and even "why" of both policies and implementation of SPP/GPP was found. The country-cases appended to the report illustrate that each country sets its own path in SPP/GPP, and that even the so-called "leaders" in SPP/GPP feel like they still have a long way to go. True integration of SPP/GPP is a long-term endeavour, one that needs nurturing and motivation in the face of many institutional barriers.

Despite the variation, some common themes also emerge that cut across the different country-level and regional experiences. While some barriers are certainly unique to a given country or region, others appear to apply across boundaries. Green and more sustainable products are still perceived — rightly or wrongly — as being more expensive than conventional alternatives, and without a strong and clear mandate to purchase them, purchasers will not overcome the requirement to choose low-cost items, without a clear legal mandatory and especially in a depressed economic environment.

Lack of clarity — even downright confusion — over determining what are the greenest products is felt by many national governments and other stakeholders, whether they are more experienced or newer to SPP/GPP. In part the confusion is a result of the success of green markets in the past five years — so many different products, claims, ecolabels and standards have been created in response to the perceived market interest in such topics that it has become a more crowded and complex marketplace for purchasers to navigate.

Both cost and complexity barriers suggest the need to develop common principles and frameworks that help purchasers to make these determinations with confidence; and to give industry the confidence to invest resources required to make this happen (beyond their marketing budgets). As green product markets scale-up, costs are likely to come down. Solving this problem is of vital importance in the overall effort to use SPP/GPP in stimulating more sustainable consumption and production systems. Looking ahead, it may well be the private sector that leads the public sector in sustainable procurement and green supply chain management. Ideally the public and private co-evolve to create a strong green economy where SPP/GPP is the norm.

There are signs that some countries are tying SPP/GPP policies to other current policy-goals, such as stimulating "green growth" and the potential competitive advantage to be gained by creating green economies, pollution prevention, the development of product standards and ecolabels. To truly reach its potential, SPP/GPP has to be embedded in other policy and market development activities, and importantly, needs to have support from decision makers in many arenas, from different of government, to industry and civil society. Those countries making advances on SPP/GPP will influence production standards around the world given the global nature of supply chains and commerce. The challenge is in implementation, and in measuring the environmental and social benefits that have been created as a result.

This review of the current state of SPP/GPP indicates the need for a set of internationally agreed and recognised principles and assessment systems for procurement sustainability, a set of indicators to monitor and evaluate SPP/GPP activities, and for capacity building with policy makers, purchasers and suppliers on how to implement SPP/GPP in a meaningful and relevant way. It is thus timely that the SPPI will address these needs as part of the 10-Year Framework Plan which has just been launched, and it is expected that this collaborative work will prove to be instrumental in accelerating and delivering on the promise of SPP/GPP worldwide.

5. References

AEA Technology (2010) Assessment and Comparison of National Green and Sustainable Public Procurement Criteria and Underlying Schemes, Report to the European Commission. See: http://ec.europa.eu/environment/gpp/pdf/Criteria%20 and%20Underlying%20Schemes.pdf

Bauer, B. Christensen, J. Christensen, K. Dyekjær-Hansen, T. and Bode, I. (2009) Benefits from Green Public Procurement. TemaNord 2009:593. Nordic Council of Ministers. Copenhagen. Available online: Benefits from Green Public Procurement. TemaNord 2009:593

Beláustegui (2011) Las compras públicas sustentables en América Latina. RICG. Programa ICT4GP/ Documento de Trabajo N° 3. Available online: http://ricg.info:8080/Plone/iniciativas-de-apoyo-es/ict4gp/grupos-de-trabajo/ttg-3-2013-compras-sustentables/documentos

Bouwer, M. Jonk, M. Szuppinger, P. Lusser, H. Berman, T. Bersani, R, Nappa, V. Viganò, C, Nissinen, A. Parikka, K. (2006) Green Public Procurement in Europe 2006. Conclusions and Recommendations. Available online: http://ec.europa.eu/ environment/gpp/pdf/take_5.pdf

Bolli, A. and Emtairah, T. (2001) Environmental benchmarking for local authorities: From concept to practice. Report prepared by International Industrial Institute for Environmental Economics. EEA. Environmental Issues Report No 20. Copenhagen. Available online: http://www.eea.europa.eu/publications/Environmental_issues_No_20/at_download/file

Brammer, S. and Walker, H. (2010) Sustainable procurement in the public sector: an international comparative study. International Journal of Operations & Production Management Vol. 31 No. 4, 2011 pp. 452-476.

Buy Smart (2011) Presentation on 14 April 2011. Available on: http://www.buy-smart.info/media/file/1163.status_quo_of_ GPP-Kaukewitsch.pdf

Centre for European Policy Studies and College of Europe (2012) The uptake of green public procurement in the EU27. Study commissioned by the European Commission. Available online: http://ec.europa.eu/environment/gpp/pdf/CEPS-CoE-GPP%20MAIN%20REPORT.pdf

Collaborating Centre on Sustainable Consumption and Production (CSCP) and The Wuppertal Institute (2007) Green Purchasing Report. CSCP/ Wuppertal Institute

Dimension Data (2011) Overcoming the challenges of green procurement through e-procurement. See: http://www.dimensiondata.com/Lists/Downloadable%20Content/ OvercomingtheChallengesofGreenProcurementThrougheProcurement_129493938599744712.pdf

EcoBuy (2009) Green Purchasing in Australia. Available online: http://www.ecobuy.org.au/director/publications/Green%20 Purchasing%20Australia%20Report.cfm

Ecolabel Index (2012) Database and Glossary, Published by Big Room Inc. Available online at: www.ecolabelindex.com

ENDS Europe (2012) Call for greener public Procurement. 18 May 2012. Available online: http://www.endseurope. com/28772/call-for-greener-public-procurement-proposal#ixzz1wHUhppl7

Environmental Development Centre (EDC) (2008) Expert Workshop on Green Public Procurement Meeting Report. Beijing, China June 11th, 2008. Available online: http://www.unep.fr/scp/marrakech/consultations/national/pdf/NatRoundtable_ China2008_FinalReportENGLISH.pdf"

European Commission (2004a) Directive 2004/17/EC (Utilities)

European Commission (2004b) Directive 2004/18/EC (Classical)

European Commission (2004c) Buying Green: A handbook for environmental public procurement. Available online: http:// ec.europa.eu/environment/gpp/pdf/buying_green_handbook_en.pdf

European Commission (2008a) COM(2008) 397 Communication on the Sustainable Consumption and Production and Sustainable Industrial Policy Action Plan

European Commission (2008b) Communication (COM (2008) 400): Public procurement for a better environment. Available online: http://ec.europa.eu/environment/gpp/what_en.htm

European Commission (2009) Clean Vehicles Directive (2009/33/EC).

European Commission (2010a) Buying Social: A Guide to Taking Account of Social Considerations in Public Procurement. Available online: http://ec.europa.eu/social/BlobServlet?docId=6457&langId=en

European Commission (2010b) National GPP Action Plans (policies and guidelines) Available online: http://ec.europa.eu/ environment/gpp/pdf/national_gpp_strategies_en.pdf

European Commission (2011) Taking stock of green public procurement in Europe. Available Online: http://ec.europa.eu/ environment/ecoap/about-eco-innovation/policies-matters/eu/743_en.htm

European Commission (2012a) Elements for a Common Strategic Framework 2014 to 2020. Brussels, 14.3.2012 SWD (2012) 61 final.

European Commission (2012b) GPP Criteria. Available Online: http://ec.europa.eu/environment/gpp/eu_gpp_criteria_en.htm

European Commission (2012c) Ecolabel and Green Public Procurement. Available Online: http://ec.europa.eu/environment/ ecolabel/ecolabel-and-green-public-procurement.html

Global Ecolabelling Network (GEN) (2009) The Role of the Thai Green Label Scheme in Thailand's Environmental Management.

Global Ecolabelling Network (GEN) (2009) Annual General Meeting Minutes (AGM) Kobe, Japan. Available online: http://www.globalecolabelling.net/docs/japan2009/09kobejapan_1-2_thailand.pdf

Giljum, S. and Polzin, C. (2009) Indicator-based evaluation of interlinkages between different sustainable development objectives (INDI-LINK). SERI for European Commission, DG Research.

Gost, R. (2011) Available online: http://www.gost-r.info/

Icelandic National Parliament (2011) Strengthening the green economy in Iceland. Althing, Reykjavik. September 2011.

ITPS (2006) Grön offentlig upphandling i Japan och USA - Lärdomar för Sverige

Ho, L. Dickinson, N. and Chan, G. (2010) Green procurement in the Asian public sector and the Hong Kong private sector. Natural Resources Forum 34.

Leire, C. Thidell, Å. and Lindhqvist, T. (2012 Forthcoming) The contribution of the Nordic Swan to GPP. TemaNord. Nordic Council of Ministers. Copenhagen.

Malumfashi, G. (2010) Green public procurement policies, climate change mitigation and international trade regulation: An assessment of the WTO Agreement on Government Procurement, Ph.D. Dissertation, University of Dundee, UK

McCrudden, (2004) Using public procurement to achieve social outcomes. Natural Resources Forum 28, pp 257-267

Michelsen, O. de Boer, L. (2009) Green procurement in Norway; a survey of practices at the municipal and county level. Journal of Environmental Management 91, 160-167.

Min, H, and Galle, W.P. (2001) Green Purchasing Practices of US firms. International Journal of Operations & Production Management, 21(9): 1222-1238.

Misiga, P. (2011) EU GPP Policies: A lever for resource efficiency. Presentation at Green Week 2011.

Morton, B. (2005) Sustainable Procurement — the national perspective. DTI-DEFRA Environmental Industries Unit and University of Manchester

Mont, O. and Leire, C. (2009) Socially Responsible Purchasing in the Supply chain. The present state in Sweden and lessons for the future. Miljöstyrningsrådet Rapport 2008:E8, SECO. Available online: http://www.msr.se/Documents/rapporter/MSR_2008_E8.pdf

Nachhaltige Kompass, 2012. Available online: http://www.kompass-nachhaltigkeit.de

New Zealand Business Council for Sustainable Development (2009) 'Sustainable Procurement in Government'. Available online: http://www.sbc.org.nz/__data/assets/pdf_file/0003/50970/Procurement-guide.pdf

Norden (2011) Ledande i grön tillväxt Rapport från de nordiska statsministrarnas arbetsgrupp för grön tillväxt. ANP 2011:717

Ochoa, A. Fuhr, V. and Gunther, D. (2003) Green purchasing in practice: experiences and new approaches from the pioneer countries. In: C. Erdmenger (Ed.) Buying into the Environment. Greenleaf Publishing, Sheffield.

OECD (2002a) Recommendation of the Council on Improving the Environmental Performance of Public Procurement. Available online: http://tinyurl.com/dxuzygs

OECD (2002b) The Size of Government Procurement Markets, OECD Journal on Budgeting, Vol. 1 No.4.

OECD (2003) The environmental performance of public procurement: the issue of policy coherence

OECD (2007) Improving the Environmental Performance of Public Procurement: Report on Implementation of the Council Recommendation.

OECD (2011) Government at a Glance 2011. ANNEX G: Detailed Data from the 2010 OECD Survey on Public Procurement . Available online: http://www.oecd-ilibrary.org/governance/government-at-a-glance-2011_gov_glance-2011-en

Oshani, P. Chowdhury, N. and Goswami, A. (2007) State of Play in Sustainable Public Procurement, IISD and TERI. Available online: http://www.iisd.org/publications/pub.aspx?id=917

PricewaterhouseCoopers (PwC), Significant and Ecofys (2009) Collection of statistical information on GPP in the EU, Report to the European Commission.

Rabbiosi, L. (2010) Ecolabelling. Presentation to OECD, Paris.

Rao, P. and Holt, D. (2005) Do green supply chains lead to competitiveness and economic performance? International Journal of Operations & Production Management, 25 (9-10), 898-916.

Sato, H. (2006) Concept and Significance of Green Purchasing Its Role, Effects, and Experiences. Presentation given at IGPN Workshop in Singapore, 2006. Available online: http://www.igpn.org/workshop/singapore/index2.html

Steurer, R., Berger, G., Konrad, A. and Martinuzzi, A. (2007) Sustainable public procurement in EU member states: overview of government initiatives and selected cases: Final Report to the EU High-Level Group on CSR, European Commission, Brussels

TemaNord (2012) Mainstreaming GPP in the Nordic Countries. Nordic Council of Ministers. TemaNord 2012:504. Available online: http://www.norden.org/sv/publikationer/publikationer/2012-504

Thomson, J. and Jackson, T. (2007) Sustainable Procurement in Practice: Lessons from Local Government Journal of

Environmental Planning and Management, Vol. 50, No. 3, 421 – 444, May 2007

UK Sustainable Procurement Task Force (2006) Procuring the Future, DEFRA, UK, June 2006. Available online: http://www.defra.gov.uk/publications/files/pb11710-procuring-the-future-060607.pdf

UN (2008) Sustainable Development Innovation Briefs Issue 5 August 2008. Public Procurement as a tool for promoting more Sustainable Consumption and Production patterns.

UN (1992) Agenda 21. Available online: http://www.un.org/esa/dsd/agenda21/

UNEP (2008) Sustainable Development Innovation Briefs. Public Procurement as a tool for promoting more Sustainable Consumption and Production patterns

UNEP (2011) Green Economy Report. Available online: http://www.unep.org/greeneconomy/

UNEP (2012) Sustainable Public Procurement Implementation Guidelines: Introducing UNEP's Approach. Available online: http://www.unep.fr/scp/procurement/docsres/ProjectInfo/UNEPImplementationGuidelines.pdf

UN Statistics Division (2012) Composition of macro geographical (continental) regions, geographical sub-regions, and selected economic and other groupings Available online: http://unstats.un.org/unsd/methods/m49/m49regin.htm

World Bank (2012) Socially Responsible Procurement. Available online: http://tinyurl.com/76nktg9

World Trade Organization (WTO) (1947) General Agreement on Tariffs and Trade (GATT) Arts. I and III. Available Online at http://www.wto.org/english/docs_e/legal_e/gatt47_01_e.htm

World Trade Organization (WTO) (2011) The plurilateral Agreement on Government Procurement (GPA) Art. III Available online at: http://www.wto.org/english/tratop_e/gproc_e/gp_gpa_e.htm

Appendix 1: Country SPP/GPP Case Studies

A. Sustainable Acquisition in the United States of America[86]

The United States Federal Government has incorporated various aspects of sustainability into its procurement practices for the last 20 years, where it is commonly referred to as "Sustainable Acquisition". The government occupies nearly 500,000 buildings, operates more than 600,000 vehicles, employs more than 1.8 million civilians, and purchases more than $500 billion per year in goods and services. As such, it is the largest single consumer in the United States, and one of the largest purchasers in the world.

The Regulatory and Policy Framework

There is currently no single overarching regulatory requirements that mandate sustainable acquisition by the government, however a mix of congressional, executive, and agency actions have supported a range of activities. The legal and policy framework for sustainable acquisition in the United States consists of:

- Statutory Requirements, such as the Resource Conservation and Recovery Act (1984), Energy Policy Act (1992, 1998, 2005), the Farm Security and Rural Investment Act (2002) and the Energy Independence and Security Act (2007); and

- Executive Requirements, including Executive Orders and other regulatory and policy requirements, such as a series of Greening of Government Executive Orders dating back to 1993 and the OMB Policy Letter 92-4 (1992).

In the last five years this activity has expanded considerably stimulated in large part by Executive Orders (EO) EO 13423[87] (2007) and EO 13514[88] (2009) which require that 95 per cent of all new contracts require products and services that are energy-efficient, water-efficient, bio-based, environmentally preferable, non-ozone depleting, contain recycled-content, or non-toxic or less-toxic alternatives, where practicable. Under the EO, all federal agencies have to submit a 2020 greenhouse gas pollution reduction target and monitor and report on their progress towards that target. The EO also directs consideration of life cycle return and costing on investment in all agency and procurement decisions.

The implementation of the EO's is overseen by the Council on Environmental Quality's Office of the federal Environmental Executive[89], which coordinates federal environmental efforts and works closely with agencies and other White House offices in the development of environmental policies and initiatives. The agency primarily responsible for the procurement of products, services and workspaces by the federal government of the United States is the General Services Administration (GSA).[90] The GSA provides office space to over one million federal employees in over 9,600 federal buildings and leases, and offers over 12 million products and services to federal agencies. The GSA has a policy to implement sustainable acquisition and has a goal to achieve a "Zero Environmental Footprint, eliminating its own impact on the natural environment, and using its government-wide influence to reduce the environmental impact of the federal government".[91]

The EPA's EPP programme[92], established pursuant to EO 12873 in 1993, developed Final Guidance for Environmentally Preferable Purchasing in 1998. This laid out the concept of multi-attribute, lifecycle-based thinking for United States government buyers for the first time. The EPP Program's approach has been to work with voluntary standards development organizations to develop comprehensive environmental performance standards in key product categories. Then, the program works with federal agencies to use these standards in their procurement. In doing so, the EPP Program has been able to use the federal government's enormous buying power to stimulate market demand for green products and services.

EPA has also supported the development of several leading ecolabels used by federal purchasers including ENERGY STAR, WaterSense and EPEAT and is actively engaged in the creation of many other environmental standards. The US Department of Agriculture has developed the BioPreferred and Organic ecolabels programs, both of which are also used in federal procurement to meet the goals of the EO.

---

86   This case was prepared with input of Alison Kinn Bennett at the US EPA.
87   http://www.gpo.gov/fdsys/pkg/FR-2007-01-26/pdf/07-374.pdf
88   http://www.gpo.gov/fdsys/pkg/FR-2009-10-08/pdf/E9-24518.pdf
89   http://www.whitehouse.gov/administration/eop/ceq
90   http://www.gsa.gov/portal/category/100000
91   http://www.gsa.gov/portal/content/184561
92   http://www.epa.gov/epp/

State and local governments in the USA operate acquisition quite independently from the federal government. However there is some informal knowledge and information sharing between agencies. Many State and Local Governments in the USA have been active in SPP/GPP and participate in member organizations, like the Responsible Purchasing Network (RPN) and the National Association of State and Local Procurement Officers (NASPO), to work together on green procurement.

One of the challenges with this approach to SPP/GPP has been that the requirements covered by these different entities have been developed independently and are therefore fragmented.

Scope

Both Executive Orders 13423 and 13514 direct federal agencies to consider the full range of environmental attributes in making procurement decisions. In addition, federal procurement already includes a number of socio-economic policy goals (e.g. preferences for small businesses, minority-owned businesses, and service-disabled veteran owned), with data collection and reporting systems in place to track government performance against these goals.

Implementation in the Procurement Cycle

Federal procurement can incorporate sustainability requirements as either preferences (rare), evaluation factors, or requirements.

Procurement personnel are held accountable on many factors, environmental and social only being two. Priorities and trade-offs among these competing procurement considerations are sometimes not clearly defined within existing law or policy.

Use of Ecolabels and Standards

Purchasers in the United States are reliant on a wide range of different standards and ecolabels (some run by the government and required, others voluntary). Recently the inter-agency Section 13 Working Group has created a robust methodology to assess ecolabels and environmental standards for use in federal procurement. The draft Guidelines are aimed at assisting the acquisition workforce in addressing many of the complexities in buying using single and multi-attribute ecolabels and standards, and will provide a consistent foundation for evaluating and utilizing them in the context of Federal procurement.

Prioritization

In order to prioritize the product and service categories of largest environmental impact, the GSA is conducting an economic input/output life cycle assessment of federal spending. Early results indicate that the following categories had the greatest environmental impact in fiscal year 2011: aircraft manufacturing, waste management and remediation services, scientific research and development services, fruit and vegetable canning, pickling and drying; and power generation and supply.

Monitoring and Reporting

Some monitoring of SPP/GPP is already happening as part of a process launched in 2009 that requires each Agency to report on their efforts with "Strategic Sustainability Performance Plans". These self-assessments are submitted annually to the President's Office of Management and Budget (OMB) who then rates using a scorecard.[93] Additional indicators to track the amount and type of SPP/GPP procurement are being developed by GSA including updating the Products and Services Code (PSC) manual to add new codes for sustainable products and services. Once complete, agencies including GSA will use the new codes to track sustainable acquisitions in contract management and reporting tools. In addition, EPA's Environmentally Preferable Purchasing Program is currently undergoing an evaluation to determine its effectiveness and impact in greening procurement and meeting a number of environmental improvement goals. The effort is demonstrating the challenges associated with assigning causality to procurement policies and product rating systems/standards for environmental outcomes that have been achieved.

---

93   Results can be viewed here: http://sustainability.performance.gov/

B. Green Public Procurement in Japan[94]

Japan has established a regulatory framework requiring implementation of green procurement by all levels of government since 2000. This framework is supported by the Green Purchasing Network, and other mechanisms including the Eco Mark ecolabel. The Basic Policy identifies and provides guidance on priority product categories. Annual reporting on the procurement of eco-friendly goods is submitted to the Minister of the Environment.

A 2010 study found that, "In Japan, the National Government and local governments spent ¥14 trillion (about US$162 billion) and ¥44 trillion (about US$510 billion), which represented 17.6 per cent of the GDP, respectively" (2005 figures).[95]

Regulatory and Policy Framework

In 2000, Japan enacted the "Law Concerning the Promotion of the Procurement of Eco-Friendly Goods and Services by the State and Other Entities", known as the Green Purchasing Law. The objectives of the law include promoting greener procurement by public institutions (government, independent administrative institutions, national universities, etc.), providing information on eco-friendly goods and services in order to reduce environmental impacts, and encouraging a shift in demand to eco-friendly goods.

In 2007, the "Law Concerning the Promotion of Contract Considering Reduction of Emissions of Greenhouse Gases and Others by the State and Other Entities", known as the Green Contract Law, was introduced as a complement to the Green Purchasing Law. The law applies to five product and service categories: electric power, automobiles, ships and vessels, energy service companies (ESCO's), and buildings, and is particularly focused on greenhouse gas reductions.

Implementation Mechanisms

Implementation of the Green Purchasing Law is the responsibility of ministries and agencies. All government bodies, including local governments (prefectures, cities, towns, villages) are required to create procurement policies and report on their procurement practices annually.

Procurement of eco-friendly goods is guided by the "Basic Policy for the Promotion of Procurement of Eco-Friendly Goods and Services", the Basic Policy. This policy includes guidance on designated, or higher priority, procurement items, the evaluation criteria for the items, and the promotion of goods meeting these criteria.

The designated procurement items list includes 246 items in 19 categories of products and services: paper, stationery, office furniture, office automation machines, mobile telephones, home electronic appliances, air conditioners, water heaters, lighting, vehicles, fire extinguishers, uniforms and work clothes, interior fixtures/bedding, work gloves, other fibre products, facilities, emergency goods, public works projects, services.

As of 2007, "…all central government ministries, 47 provisional governments, 12 designated cities and 68 per cent of 700 cities practicing green procurement are obliged to comply, and cumulatively, 95 per cent of all purchased products in the designated categories are "green products".[96]

Information from manufacturers and environmental labelling organizations is managed and analysed by the government of Japan. Using this information, guidelines and criteria are established to facilitate implementation of this law and associated procurement policies.

Promotion of green markets, products, and services is through organizations such as the Green Purchasing Network (GPN) (established in 1996). Established with the support of the Ministry of Environment, the 2577 member GPN[97] includes private sector firms, government agencies, consumer associations, and NGOs. Under its mandate, the GPN develops tools, conducts research, maintains a database of 15,023 products[98], and promotes green procurement in both government and private sector contexts.

---

94   This case was prepared with input from Akira Kataoka of the International Green Purchasing Network.
95   Ho et al, 2010.
96   Ho et al, 2010.
97   As at March 2012.
98   As at May 2012.

The Use of Ecolabels and Standards

Since 1989, the Japanese "Eco Mark" programme has been operated by Japan Environment Association (JEA) as a means of supporting greener procurement. A Type I (ISO 14020) ecolabel, Eco Mark is a widely used indicator of environmentally preferable products in Japan. Currently, Eco Mark has 5,148 certified products in 51 categories.[99] Other sources of product criteria serving as a reference for government purchasers include ENERGY STAR and other criteria databases specially designed to support the government green procurement.[100]

Challenges and Looking Forward for Japan

In sub-national government, implementation of the Green Purchasing Law has been uneven, due to a lack of understanding and awareness of green procurement. Where it is implemented, focus is on office products and ecolabelled goods.

Areas for attention include the integration of social and ethical components of public procurement into sustainable procurement policies, analysis of impacts of procurement policies, and lifecycle costing. In 2012, the International Green Purchasing Network secretariat and the Green Purchasing Network initiated a series of workshops on the development of procurement guidelines incorporating ethical and corporate social responsibility factors.

---

99   As at April 2012.
100   As at April 2012.

C. Sustainable Purchasing in Chile[101]

Chile continues to work to integrate sustainability into its procurement practices, in line with an overall trend toward integrating environmental practices into public policy. The Public Procurement and Contracting Bureau — also know as ChileCompra or Dirección ChileCompra — operates under the supervision of the President of the Republic through the Ministry of Finance. ChileCompra oversees US$8 billion in annual transactions, accounting for more than 3.2 per cent of Chile's GDP. Notably, ChileCompra set a target of 15 per cent of procurement orders meeting sustainability criteria by the end of 2012. According to ChileCompra this target was met one year early, with 17.2 per cent of purchase orders including sustainability criteria by the end of 2011, up from 1.3 per cent in 2009. This was achieved through a combination of policy changes, ecolabel integration, provider accreditation, training and capacity building.

Regulatory and Policy Framework

The Law on Procurement (No. 19,886) provides scope for a life-cycle approach to public procurement in Article 6, where it states that:

> "The bidding specifications must establish the conditions that allow for the most advantageous combination between the benefits of goods or services to be purchased and all their present and future related costs."[102]

The Law is viewed as providing enough flexibility to implement sustainability procurement practices over time and using a sector or factor based approach. For example, in March 2008 Procurement Policy No. 9 provided guidance on the evaluation of offers for all products that use energy to operate. Buyers were advised to prefer products classified as 'efficient'. Specifically, of products that carried an energy efficient label with rankings from A (most efficient) to G (least efficient), preference was recommended for products bearing higher ratings of A to C. Buyers were also advised to consider the full useful life and life cycle of the products.[103] A procurement manual accompanied the Policy and provided further guidance on procuring energy efficient products, including reference to the ENERGY STAR ecolabel.

- Guidance notes have also been released covering:
- Key sustainability concepts in public procurement
- Socially responsible public procurement
- Sustainability criteria in defence procurement
- Sustainability criteria in Ministry of Housing and Urban Development procurement

Implementation in the Procurement Cycle

Chile's e-procurement system, which comprises electronic platforms such as www.mercadopublico.cl (including ChileCompra Express), and the Electronic Registry of State Suppliers, have been key to Chile meeting its sustainable procurement targets. Training, accreditation, ecolabel integration and information sharing were all enabled by this platform. Indeed, it appears that implementation of e-government in this case did not only yield cost savings, it also resulted in sustainability benefits. For example, in 2012 ChileCompra introduced an e-learning course on concepts of social responsibility in public procurement.[104]

Use of Ecolabels and Standards

ChileCompra Express, which accounts for 18 per cent of all public procurement transactions in Chile (2011), is where the bulk of ecolabel-based sustainable procurement practice is put into action. According to ChileCompra, ChileCompra Express includes support for suppliers to designate their products with the following ecolabels: PEFC, FSC, and ENERGY STAR. In 2011, about 29 per cent — 432 out of about 1,500 — of the suppliers on ChileCompra Express received the highest environmental/social score.[105]

Also according to ChileCompra, as of 2012, 58 per cent of the products, services and companies listed on ChileCompra Express have "sustainable seals". However, significant sector gaps remain where no ecolabel coverage is available.[106]

---

101   This case was prepared with input from Pablo A. Prüssing Fuchslocher from Dirección ChileCompra.

102   Public Procurement Law No. 19,886: http://www.chilecompra.cl/index.php?option=com_phocadownload&view=category&download=6 59%3Aley-de-compras-publicas-no-19.886&id=10%3Anormativa-de-compras-pblicas&Itemid=548&lang=es

103   Procurement Policy No. 9, 2008: http://www.comprassustentables.cl/index.php?option=com_phocadownload&view=category&downl oad=2:directiva-de-contratacion-publica-nd9-2008&id=2:documentos&Itemid=2

104   http://www.comprassustentables.cl/index.php?option=com_content&view=article&id=58:chilecompra-promueve-conceptos-de-responsabilidad-social-en-compradores-publicos-&catid=6:noticias&Itemid=8

105   http://www.comprassustentables.cl/index.php?option=com_content&view=article&id=43:pnuma-desarrollo-taller-regional-sobre-eco-etiquetado-en-el-cono-sur-&catid=6:noticias&Itemid=8

106   http://www.comprassustentables.cl/index.php?option=com_lyftenbloggie&view=entry&year=2012&month=05&day=31&id=12%3Achile compra-express-mercado-electronico-sostenible&Itemid=3

Prioritization

Capacity building for micro, small and medium enterprise is a priority for ChileCompra. Sustainable procurement is viewed in the context of free trade agreements, where SMEs and environmental regulations are often considered. High-level guidance an implementation monitoring at an international level is important, as is direct contact between countries, via workshops and training. Building trust and long-term relationships will be key to developing the field of sustainable procurement in Chile and internationally.

Monitoring and Reporting

Strengthening monitoring and reporting are potential next steps for Chile in the field of sustainable procurement. Under consideration is monitoring the percentage and number of products being bought using environmental criteria and where possible mapped to cost and/or environmental savings would be a useful tool in tracking performance. The percentage of procurement orders meeting sustainability criteria could also continue to be tracked over time.

D. Green Public Procurement in the European Union[107]

The potential of purchasing power to realize environmental (and social) improvements is widely acknowledged in the European Union (EU). Central governments, regional and local authorities among the EU Member States started to work with green procurement in the nineties. Green Public Procurement (GPP) was first mentioned as a European Commission (EC) policy instrument in the Integrated Product Policy (IPP) from 2003 and was shortly thereafter acknowledged in the Public Procurement Directives of 2004. An "Interpretative Communication" and also court cases provided clarification about the legal possibility to include environmental and social considerations in procurement. Currently, the Communication 'Public procurement for a better environment' (COM (2008) 400) is the guiding document on how the public sector can use GPP to reduce its environmental impact and to stimulate innovation in environmental technologies, products and services.

EU public procurers spend over £2,000 billion[108] on supplies, works, and services every year; this is equivalent to approximately 17 per cent of GDP in the EU.[109] GPP is gaining momentum also in EU strategy documents, such as in the flagship initiatives 'Road Map to Resource Efficient Europe' for the Europe 2020 Strategy[110], which states that by 2020, market and policy incentives are in place that reward business investment in efficiency. This should be accomplished with measures to, "strengthen the requirements on Green Public Procurement (GPP) for products with significant environmental impacts; assess where GPP could be linked to EU funded projects; and promote joint procurement, and networks of public procurement officers in support of GPP." GPP is also referred to in a number of other EC strategy and policy documents.[111]

In 2008, the EC set an indicative target that by 2010, 50 per cent of all public tendering procedures should be "green" for ten priority products and services.[112] However, though some progress has been made, a recent study has shown that this target has not been met.[113]

Regulatory and Policy Framework

Public procurement is mainly regulated by two separate EU Directives: Directive 2004/18 focuses on contracting authorities ("Classical Directive"); and Directive 2004/17 which is oriented towards entities operating in the water, energy, transport and postal services sectors ("utilities directive"). The Directives stipulate transparent procedures and provide for fair market conditions for the suppliers in line with the rules of the European Single Market. The Directives provides the scope of possible action for GPP in the EU, even if they do not prescribe GPP. They do mention that environmental and social considerations may be included in subject matter, technical specifications, selection and award criteria, and contract performance clauses.[114] For the individual Member State, procurement contracts above certain thresholds are subject to the Directives; contracts below are subject to national regulation.[115]

Also other EU Directives and legislation ask for obligatory use of GPP[116], such as the Clean Vehicle Directive[117] and ENERGY STAR.[118] In addition, there are minimum legal requirements for the purchasing of timber.[119]

The Commission's Joint Research Centre's Institute for Prospective Technological Studies (JRC-IPTS) in Seville, Spain is leading the criteria development process on the basis of an annual ecolabel/GPP work plan.[120] This work plan is adopted in consultation with the informal GPP Advisory Group: a consultative body established 2010 for general policy

---

107   This case was prepared with input from Alenka Burja, Ministry of the Agriculture and Environment, Slovenia and Robert Kaukewitsch, EU DG Environment.

108   EC. 2010. DG MARKT ROADMAP. Modernization of EU public procurement rules. Available on http://ec.europa.eu/governance/impact/planned_ia/docs/2011_markt_017_public_procurement_en.pdf

109   European Commission. 2010 COMMUNICATION FROM THE COMMISSION TO THE EUROPEAN PARLIAMENT, THE COUNCIL, THE ECONOMIC AND SOCIAL COMMITTEE AND THE COMMITTEE OF THE REGIONS Towards a Single Market Act For a highly competitive social market economy: 50 proposals for improving our work, business and exchanges with one another. COM(2010) 608 final.

110   Europe 2020 Strategy: A European strategy for smart, sustainable and inclusive growth, se Elements for a Common Strategic Framework 2014 to 2020. Brussels, 14.3.2012 SWD (2012) 61 final. Commission Staff Document. Available on http://ec.europa.eu/environment/gpp/eu_policy_en.htm

111   For example, public procurement as an important tool for boosting the uptake of environmental technologies is mentioned the EU Environmental Technologies Action Plan (ETAP). More information on legislation to be taken into account for EU GPP policies can be found on http://ec.europa.eu/environment/gpp/eu_related_en.htm

112   Public Procurement for a better environment. Com (2008) 400 final.

113   http://ec.europa.eu/environment/gpp/index_en.htm and http://ec.europa.eu/environment/gpp/studies_en.htm

114   McCrudden, 2004.

115   Also other parts are (partially) excluded from the directives, e.g. defence. Moreover, the general treaty principles (equal treatment, non-discrimination, transparency etc.) also apply below the thresholds.

116   http://ec.europa.eu/environment/gpp/eu_related_en.htm

117   http://ec.europa.eu/transport/urban/index_en.htm

118   http://www.dcenr.gov.ie/Energy/Energy+Efficiency+and+Affordability+Division/Energy+Star+Regulation.htm

119   http://europa.eu/legislation_summaries/environment/nature_and_biodiversity/ev0018_en.htm

120   http://ec.europa.eu/environment/ecolabel/about_ecolabel/pdf/work_plan.pdf

issues and for the development of EU GPP criteria. The GPP Advisory Group is composed of one representative per Member State as well as four representatives of other stakeholders (i.e. civil society, industry, SMEs, public procurement and local authorities).

EU funding is also provided to the ICLEI Procura+ campaign, which advises and supports local authorities and provides information on GPP, such as the "Procura+ Manual" with guidance and criteria[121] to public authorities.

Scope and Product Categories

Ten priority sectors have been identified for greening the public procurement in the 2008 EU GPP Communication: Construction; Food and catering services; Transport and transport services; Energy; Office machinery and computers; Clothing, uniforms and other textiles; Paper and printing services; Furniture; Cleaning products and services; and Equipment used in the health sector.[122] As of 2010, the product groups covered by national GPP efforts in nine EU Member States and Norway are shown in the table below.[123]

GPP in Europe	AT	BE	DK	FI	FR	DE	NL	NO	SE	UK
Copying and graphic paper	✔	✔	✔	✔	✔	✔	✔	✔	✔	✔
Cleaning products/ services	✔	✔	✔	✔	✔		✔	✔	✔	✔
Office IT and equipment	✔	✔	✔	✔	✔	✔	✔	✔	✔	✔
Construction	✔	✔	✔		✔		✔	✔	✔	✔
Transport	✔	✔	✔		✔		✔	✔	✔	✔
Furniture	✔	✔	✔	✔	✔		✔	✔	✔	✔
Electricity	✔						✔	✔	✔	
Food and catering services	✔	✔			✔		✔	✔	✔	
Textiles	✔	✔	✔		✔		✔	✔	✔	✔

Table 4: European Product Category Guidelines

In the EU, common GPP Criteria have been developed for purchasers with the purpose to help avoid a distortion of the European single market, to enhance EU-wide competition, trigger new green markets and development of new environmental technologies and greener products and services, and to reduce administrative burden.[124] The EU GPP Criteria documents are based on available scientific information and data (including ecolabelling), a life-cycle approach and stakeholder engagement. Two levels of stringency are provided: core criteria that are designed to allow easy application of GPP; and comprehensive criteria — which take include more ambitious requirements and/or include a greater number of aspects of environmental performance.[125] To date, the Commission has developed common GPP Criteria for 19 product groups[126] and several others are currently in development.[127] In addition to the GPP Criteria, guidelines on GPP practices are provided in the "Buying Green Handbook".[128]

Social and ethical aspects are also increasingly considered as many public procurement authorities embed GPP in a broader approach to sustainability.[129] However, most guidelines and studies in the EU so far have focused on environmental or green aspects.[130] The inclusion of social aspects in other stages of the procurement process is addressed in "Buying Social" guide[131] and in the report of the Standing Forestry Committee ad hoc Working Group IV on "Public procurement of wood and wood-based products".[132]

121　The product groups for which the manual provides criteria are construction, IT, cleaning products, food, buses and electricity.
122　European Commission, 2008.
123　AEA, 2010.
124　http://ec.europa.eu/environment/gpp/gpp_criteria_en.htm
125　Assessment and Comparison of National Green and Sustainable Public Procurement Criteria and Underlying Schemes.
126　http://ec.europa.eu/environment/gpp/eu_gpp_criteria_en.htm
127　Upcoming product groups are for example taps and showerheads, waste water treatment plants, toilets and urinals.
128　http://ec.europa.eu/environment/gpp/buying_handbook_en.htm
129　http://ec.europa.eu/environment/gpp/versus_en.htm
130　Steurer et al, 2007. Sustainable Public Procurement in EU Member States: Overview of government initiatives and selected cases Final Report to the EU High-Level Group on CSR.
131　Buying Social: A Guide to Taking Account of Social Considerations in Public Procurement.
132　http://ec.europa.eu/agriculture/fore/publi/index_en.htm

The newly proposed procurement directives (December 2011) underline the possibility to consider lifecycle cost (LCC) in procurement.[133] Lifecycle costs are typically taken into account in awarding contracts based on the most economically advantageous tender.[134] The conventional LCC techniques most widely used by companies and/or governments are purely financial and assess investment, operation, maintenance and end-of-life disposal expenses.[135]

Implementation Status

The IPP communication from 2003 called on the Member States to create National Action Plans (NAPs) including assessment and targets. The NAPs are not legally binding, although if Member States want to, they can be binding, and allow Member States to choose the options that best suit their political framework and the level they have reached. To date, most of the EU Member States have adopted a NAP. The extent to which the countries have developed tools for implementation differs widely, as illustrated in the table below which shows the status quo of GPP policy tools in Europe in 2010.[136] In addition, a number of additional EU Member States have since established NAPs or decrees, such as Ireland and Slovenia.

GPP element	Implementation
GPP - Legally binding (selected focus areas)	3 Member States: PT, DE, CZ
National Action Plan or equivalent document adopted	21 Member States: AT, BE, CY, CZ, DK, FI, FR, DE, IT, LV, LT, LU, MT, NL, PO, PT, SK, SI, ES, SE, UK
NAP in process of preparation	6 Member States: BG, EE, GR, IE, HU, RO
Targets/criteria adopted	21 Member States
Market analysis conducted	9 Member States
Communication/dissemination activities	9 Member States
Training activities	18 Member States
Monitoring	11 Member States

The EC's GPP website offers a range of tools for procuring entities. A helpdesk for GPP, launched in 2010, promotes and disseminates information about GPP, and provides timely and accurate answers to stakeholders' enquiries.[137] The European Commission also offers nearly 50 examples/good practices of GPP implementation coming from all member states, monthly GPP news and alerts.[138]

Monitoring and Reporting

GPP is a voluntary instrument and monitoring/reporting by the Member States is not mandatory. Nevertheless, studies have been conducted to measure the uptake of GPP practices among a number of the Member States. The most recent EC study is from 2011[139], in which over 850 public authorities from 26 Member States provided information on their use of core GPP criteria in the last contract they had signed for one of the ten prioritized product/service groups. The respondents also gave more general information on the "greenness" of their overall procurement in the period 2009/2010 regarding a total of more than 230,000 contracts signed, for a value of approximately 117.5 billion Euros. The study shows that 26 per cent of the contracts signed in the period included all of the studied core GPP criteria; however, 55 per cent of the contracts included at least one EU core GPP criterion. It also found that some form of green procurement is being incorporated at a large scale, and that the longitudinal results within the studied period points towards positive trend. Moreover, the uptake of EU GPP criteria varies significantly across Europe, with four top performing countries (Belgium, Denmark, Netherlands and Sweden), in which all EU core GPP criteria were applied in 40-60 per cent of the cases.[140]

---

133   http://ec.europa.eu/internal_market/publicprocurement/modernising_rules/reform_proposals_en.htm

134   An example of how environmental externalities may be included in LCC is given by the Clean Vehicles Directive (2009/33/EC). Under this Directive, contracting authorities and entities are obliged to take energy consumption and emissions into account in their purchases of road transport vehicles.

135   http://ec.europa.eu/environment/gpp/lcc.htm

136   http://ec.europa.eu/environment/gpp/action_plan_en.htm

137   http://ec.europa.eu/environment/gpp/helpdesk.htm

138   http://ec.europa.eu/environment/gpp/

139   http://ec.europa.eu/environment/gpp/studies_en.htm

140   CEPS and College of Europe, 2012

E. Green Public Procurement in India[141]

The use of public procurement as an instrument to influence the market trends in favour of environmentally and socially responsible products and services is relatively a new concept in India. However, different elements of environmental sustainability feature in and influence the procurement choices across governments and suppliers.[142] The setting is conducive for adopting sustainable purchasing as an environmental policy instrument in a more structured way.

Regulatory and Policy Frameworks

Public procurement in India has been estimated to constitute about 30 per cent of GDP.[143] There is no procurement law to date and public procurement in India is governed through government policies. General Financial Rules (GFR) lays down basic principles of efficiency, economy, transparency, fairness and equitability and promotion of competition in procurement to be followed by central government departments/agencies. There is provision of judicial review of executive's decision to reduce arbitrariness.

Recent Developments on Green Public Procurement

In 2011, The Ministry of Environment and Forest, Government of India nominated a committee to formulate guidelines on Green Public Procurement. The committee has recommended legislation to establish the necessary provisions and institutional arrangement for encouraging central government to procure greener products and services. Recently, the Government of India has introduced Draft Public Procurement Bill-2012, which states "evaluation criteria shall relate to the subject matter of procurement and may include - (a) the price; (b) the cost of operating, maintaining and repairing goods or works…, the characteristics of the subject matter of procurement, such as the functional characteristics of goods or works and the environmental characteristics of the subject matter…". This law, once enacted, would provide legitimacy to a procurers' decisions of integrating environmental concerns in public buying.

Ecolabels and Environmental Standards

Since its release in 1996, ISO 14001 has emerged as the leading voluntary system for certifying a firm's commitment to environmental management.[144] However, the use of ecolabel and environmental standards in procurement of products, works and services is not very common. Ecomark, the Indian ecolabel for products, was introduced in 1991 but the label has so far had a low uptake from both manufacturers and buyers.[145]

Challenges and Looking Ahead

The critical issues facing greater uptake of GPP in India include: limited political motivation; the absence of a clear legal framework and guidelines; a lack of knowledge to avoid legal and technical problems during the procurement process (inclusion, evaluation and monitoring); limited knowledge of and experience in using tools such as LCC and LCA; a dependency on experts to define specifications; and the perceived higher costs of greener products. Vendors advocate for SPP/GPP to be implemented in a transparent way with sufficient time to react; that Intellectual Property Rights are respected and that product quality is guaranteed by third party certification.

Implementation of SPP/GPP in practice would require not only laws and guidelines, but also a change in attitude amongst producers and consumers. A shift towards understanding that spending public money is an opportunity to directly foster sustainable development and innovation is needed. This calls for capacity building of all stakeholders. Equipping public buyers with the know-how on how to include sustainability requirements into their purchasing processes would be a key to successful implementation of SPP/GPP.

---

141 This case was prepared with input from Sanjay Kumar, Indian Railways.
142 IISD, 2008, Sustainable Public Procurement: Towards a low carbon economy.
143 OECD, 2011.
144 Samir A. Qadir and Hugh S. Gorman (2008). The Use of ISO 14001 in India: More Than a Certificate on the Wall? Environmental Practice, 10 , pp 53-65 doi:10.1017/S1466046608080174.
145 IISD, 2008, Sustainable Public Procurement: Towards a low carbon economy.

F: Mandatory Green Public Procurement in Slovenia[146]

GPP work began in Slovenia in 2008, when a working group on GPP was set-up within the National Council on Sustainable Development. The working group was led by the Government Office for Growth, and consisted of various stakeholders such as governmental bodies, representatives from industry (Chamber of Commerce), local communities, and civil society. The Ministry of Finance now leads the GPP effort. Other institutions involved with the promotion, implementation and preparation of GPP legislation and criteria are the Ministry of Agriculture and Environment and the Ministry of Economic Development and Technology.

Regulatory and Policy Framework

The Slovenian National Action Plan (NAP) on GPP was developed by the Working Group on GPP and was adopted by the Slovenian Government on 21st of May 2009.[147] The key target is to achieve in average 50 per cent of GPP by 2012 by all public contracting authorities for eight products categories. NAP provided a legal ground for a Decree on GPP, which was adopted in December 2011.

The measures adopted in NAP include: preparation and adoption of a Decree on GPP; adoption of legislation regarding reporting obligations about GPP implementation; promotion of the NAP and training of purchasers on how to use GPP criteria; establishment of a GPP portal; execution of some pilot GPP projects; dialog with the business sector and preparation for follow-up analysis of the market; and the introduction of environmental management system in the public sector.

Scope

The NAP on GPP outlines general system goals and sets indicators for eight product categories, namely paper, electricity, IT office equipment, furniture, transport, food and catering, construction, cleaning products and services. Product categories were chosen based on the frequency and scope of public procurement of products and services; potential for reduction of environmental impacts by introducing GPP criteria; the level of complexity of GPP criteria; and also based on outcomes of a market analysis study completed showing the potential availability of greener products/ services in the Slovene market that could meet GPP criteria.

The Decree[148] and NAP on GPP covers environmental criteria and at this time no social or broader sustainability criteria are included.

Implementation

GPP is mandatory for all public bodies in Slovenia to follow, including state, local and other public agencies.

The Decree[149] on GPP sets minimal mandatory environmental requirements, which must be considered when awarding a public contract, and recommendations to achieve higher environmental standards. Currently, the decree covers environmental criteria for 11 groups of products and services (electricity, food and catering services, copying and tissue paper, IT office equipment, audio and video equipment, household appliances and air-conditioning devices, construction of buildings, furniture, cleaning products and services and laundry services, road vehicles and tyres). Slovenian GPP criteria is based on the EU GPP criteria and relevant legislation taking into account the capacities of Slovenian public contracting authorities, the market and current economic situation. Updating and upgrading of current criteria and adoption of environmental criteria for new product and service groups is envisaged in the future.

Contracting authorities must consider GPP criteria during the assessment of needs, and must include them in the tender documentation when inviting potential suppliers to submit a bid. In tender documentation, contracting authorities must include the environmental aspect already when formulating the Subject Matter of a particular call, and the GPP criteria are included by setting relevant technical specifications, selection criteria, award criteria and/or contractual clauses. Life cycle costing (LCC) is currently used in vehicle procurement.

There is no national Type I ecolabel programme in Slovenia, however the EU Ecolabel, among other equivalent labels is used as a reference for product category criteria, and EMAS and ISO 14001 Standards for environmental management systems are also considered.

---

146   This case was prepared with input from Alenka Burja, Ministry of the Agriculture and Environment, Slovenia.

147   Slovenian NAP on GPP, see: http://www.mf.gov.si/fileadmin/mf.gov.si/pageuploads/javnar/UredbaZelenJN/Akcijski_ZeJN.PDF

148   Decree on Green Public Procurement (Official Gazette no. 102/2011, 18/2012 and 24/2012), see: http://www.uradni-list.si/1/objava.jsp ?urlid=2011102&stevilka=4404; and http://www.uradni-list.si/1/objava.jsp?urlid=201218&stevilka=730

149   http://www.uradni-list.si/1/objava.jsp?urlid=201224&stevilka=1000. The unofficial consolidated Sloveninan text of the decree is also available at: http://www.mf.gov.si/si/delovna_podrocja/sistem_javnega_narocanja/predpisi/ - Neuradno precišceno besedilo Uredbe o zelenem javnem narocanju št. 2.

Monitoring and Evaluation

As a mandatory requirement, implementation of GPP is followed-up through collection of statistical data on public procurement.[150] Monitoring is facilitated by the availability of electronic publication of notices.

For example, recent monitoring analysed the GPP criteria applied within the number and value of all public procurement contracts and awarded within a certain calendar year. In 2009, 415 green public procurement contracts were awarded. Their value is 246,32 mio EUR. This represents 8.89 per cent of total value of Slovene public procurement in 2009, and 8.71 per cent of all public procurement procedures carried out in 2009.

---

150   The latest report on GPP implementation is available at http://www.mf.gov.si/fileadmin/mf.gov.si/pageuploads/javnar/Porocilo_AN_ZeJN_NOVO_18_5.pdf

Appendix 2: International Initiatives on SPP/GPP

Recognising the potential for SPP/GPP to contribute to sustainable economic development, various international and regional organizations and networks have been launched to promote SPP/GPP. ICLEI's "Sustainable Procurement Resource Centre" lists some 62 tools and initiatives on SPP/GPP from around the world, though many of these are projects that have now come to completion. Nevertheless, there is a wealth of information available online, covering:

- Awareness-raising and education on what is SPP and the benefits of SPP/GPP;
- Toolkits and "how to" guides;
- Explanation of legal and policy requirements;
- Product specific guidelines (see overview below);
- Sample specification and contract language;
- Calculators and measurement tools;
- Training and capacity-building;
- References and reports; and
- Links to other information sources and initiatives.

A brief description of international SPP/GPP initiatives is provided below, followed by a mapping of product specific guidance provided by some of the initiatives. There are many other national, sector specific and regional initiatives not covered here, each serving more specific audiences.

Compass Sustainability Platform

Website: http://kmu.kompass-nachhaltigkeit.ch/about.html

BSD Consulting, ITC, and SECO created the German and French language Compass Sustainability platform, which serves to help professional purchasers and SME suppliers navigate sustainability standards and guide them in sustainable procurement. The platform shows the steps to implement sustainable procurement and green supply chain management; and shows SME's how to meet those criteria mandated by procurers and sustainability standards. It provides an overview of sustainable procurement and links to other information resources.

European Commission GPP

Website: http://ec.europa.eu/environment/gpp/index_en.htm

The European Commission GPP website, managed by DG Environment, contains criteria, guidance, case studies, training and research on SPP from across Europe. Guidance initiatives include the GPP Toolkit (with training material on GPP), summaries of EU countries' integration of GPP into their National Action Plans, product guidelines and criteria, The Buy Green Handbook, the Buy Social Handbook and the GPP Helpdesk (managed by ICLEI).

International Green Purchasing Network - IGPN

Website: http://www.igpn.org/

The International Green Purchasing Network was established in 2006, and the Japanese Green Purchasing Network acts as its Secretariat. Its mission is to promote GPP by coordinating those organizations who are implementing or supporting GPP activities. Members of the IGPN are primarily national green purchasing networks in Asia (including Green Purchasing Networks of China, Hong Kong, India, Indonesia Japan, Republic of Korea, Malaysia, The Philippines, Singapore, Taiwan, Thailand, Viet Nam). IGPN promotes green purchasing around the world, and its website contains criteria, links, news and events. It produces the freely available Green Purchasing and Green Public Procurement Starter Kit, and an interactive web and CD-ROM based package which providing information in interactive modules, available in Chinese, English, Thai and Vietnamese.

IISD – Programme on Sustainable Public Procurement

Website: http://www.iisd.org/markets/procurement/country_projects.asp

The International Institute for Sustainable Development (IISD) supports the design and implementation of SPP/GPP in developing and emerging countries. IISD has advised a number of governments on the design and implementation of sustainable procurement policies, including India, South Africa, the United States of America, Canada (Province of Manitoba), Chile, Viet Nam, Brazil, China, Abu Dhabi and Ghana. This work-stream is expanding in 2012 to examine the application of SPP/GPP within fragile states. IISD also works on public-private partnerships (PPPs) as a vehicle for sustainable development, and a multi-stakeholder initiative demonstrating procurement as an accelerator of "green growth".

NAGPI – Commission for Environmental Cooperation

Website: http://www.cec.org/Page.asp?PageID=924&SiteNodeID=605&AA_SiteLanguageID=1

The North American Green Purchasing Initiative (NAGPI) is a project of the Commission for Environmental Cooperation, an inter-governmental agency for Canada, the USA and Mexico that facilitates collaboration and public participation to foster conservation, protection and enhancement of the North American environment. NAGPI plays a coordinating role to compile and maintain information on GPP to avoid duplicated efforts, create a unified voice to engage stakeholder, and develops and maintain a database of supporting tools and policies in North America.

OECD Guidance on GPP

Website: http://www.oecd.org/document/21/0,3343,en_2649_34281_37414933_1_1_1_1,00.html

Since 1996, the OECD has provided research, analysis and recommendations on GPP for member countries through workshops and policy reviews, as well as analysis of the institutional factors that facilitate or hinder success in GPP. Recent work has focused on the links between the environmental characteristics of public procurement and other aspects of public policy such as general environmental policy, public expenditure management, trade law and competition policy. An OECD Council Recommendation in 2002[151] urges member governments to provide appropriate policy frameworks and support for GPP, and calls upon member countries "to take concrete steps to ensure the incorporation of environmental criteria into public procurement of products and services." Recommended actions include establishing appropriate procedures for the identification of greener products, government-wide information, training and technical assistance to facilitate implementation, and the development of indicators to monitor and evaluate programmes and policies.

Procura+ Campaign – ICLEI

Website: http://www.procuraplus.org/

ICLEI (The International Council on Local Environmental Initiatives), an international association of local and regional local government organizations in 2004 launched Procura+, managed by ICLEI's European Secretariat. Procura+ has the goals of supporting public authorities in implementing sustainable public procurement, promoting achievements of public authorities internationally, and fostering exchange on good practice from public procurers and experts internationally. Procura+ has many members and expert partners, and provides information in several different (mostly European) languages. ICLEI and Procura+ are also commissioned by the European Commission to run the "GPP Help Desk" and produce guidance documents for European public procurers on GPP. ICLEI also produces a comprehensive online resource and platform on SPP, the Sustainable Procurement Resource Centre.

Responsible Purchasing Network (RPN)

Website: http://www.responsiblepurchasing.org/

The Responsible Purchasing Network (RPN) is an international network of buyers dedicated to socially responsible and environmentally sustainable purchasing. Its primary focus is North American state and local government procurement officers.

Sustainable Public Procurement Initiative (SPPI)

Website: http://www.unep.fr/scp/procurement/

UNEP promotes sustainable public procurement through the Sustainable Public Procurement Initiative (SPPI). The SPPI is an evolution of work undertaken for the Marrakesh Task Force on SPP, which developed a specific methodology to implement SPP/GPP. UNEP piloted the approach in seven countries (Lebanon, Mauritius, Colombia, Chile, Costa Rica, Chile, Uruguay). The SPPI facilitates global consensus on the integration of sustainable development considerations in procurement at all levels (UN, national governments and local authorities); fosters information exchange, and provides practical tools for capacity building to translate sustainable procurement policies into reality.

Sustainable United Nations (SUN) and Greening the Blue

Website: http://www.greeningtheblue.org/resources/procurement

The UN also has an internal initiative for making its own agencies' purchases more sustainable, as coordinated by the Sustainable UN Facility (SUN). Material prepared for this programme, including product guides, guides on using ecolabels and standards, trainings and monitoring reports are posted on the Greening the Blue website.

---

151   OECD, 2002a.

Appendix 3: Expert Interviewees, Reviewers and Survey Pilot Organizations

We would like to very much thank the following experts for their input, also all of the participants who completed the survey.

Interviewees
Conducted in May and June 2012:
- Abby Semple, Independent / ICLEI, UK
- Akira Kataoka, International Green Purchasing Network (IGPN) Secretariat, Japan
- Alenka Burja, Ministry of Agriculture and Environment, Slovenia
- Alison Kinn Bennett, Environmental Protection Authority, USA
- Augustine Koh, Malaysian Green Purchasing Network, Malaysia
- Barbara Morton, Sustainable Procurement Ltd, UK
- Carlos Andrés Enmanuel, UNEP DTIE, France
- Farid Yaker, UNEP DTIE, France
- Ian Barhman, DEFRA, UK
- Mats Ekenger, Nordic Council of Ministers, Denmark
- Miguel Porrúa, Organization of American States, USA
- Niels Ramm, UNOPS, Denmark
- Pablo A. Prüssing Fuchslocher, Dirección ChileCompra, Chile
- Peter Nohrstedt, SEMCO, Sweden
- Robert Kaukewitsch, European Commission, Belgium
- Sanjay Kumar, Indian Railways, India

Draft Survey and Report Reviewers
- Akira Kataoka, IGPN, Japan
- Alenka Burja Ministry of Agriculture and Environment, Slovenia
- Alison Kinn Bennett, Environmental Protection Authority, USA
- Barbara Morton, Sustainable Procurement Ltd, UK
- Dr. Carl Dalhammar, IIIEE Lund University, Sweden
- Dr. Handito Joewono, Green Purchasing Network, Indonesia
- Jacob Malthouse, Big Room Inc., Canada
- Jason Pearson, Sustainable Purchasing Council, USA
- Maria Sundesten, The Nordic Swan, Sweden
- Norma Tregurtha, ISEAL Alliance, UK
- Peter Nohrstedt, SEMCO, Sweden
- Robert Kaukewitsch, European Commission, Belgium
- Sylvain Chevassus, Ministère de l'écologie, du développement durable et de l'énergie, France
- Sanjay Kumar, Indian Railways, India
- Trevor Bowden, Big Room Inc., Canada
- Yalmaz Siddiqui, Office Depot, USA
- Zuzana Baranovicová, Slovenská agentúra životného prostredia, Slovakia

Pilot Survey Respondents
- Aure Adell, Ecoinstitut, Spain
- Bettina Schaefer, Ecoinstitut, Spain
- Helena Fonseca, Organization of American States, USA
- Jerry Sebastian Ackotia, Public Procurement Authority, Ghana
- Sanjay Kumar, Indian Railways, India
- Scot Case, UL Environment, USA
- Shirley Soto Montero, Ministerio de Ambiente, Energía y Telecomunicaciones, Costa Rica
- Tahalooa Sacheedanand, Ministry of Finance, Mauritius
- Thad Carlson, Best Buy Co., Inc., USA

Appendix 4: Organizations whose Members Participated in the Survey

In some cases more than one person responded from the same organization; in the following table each organization is listed once.

Organization	Country
ACCORD3.0	USA
Achieving Health Nigeria Initiative	Nigeria
ACRA	Italy
ADEME	France
African Development Bank	Tunisia
Agence de l'Environment et du Développement Durable (AEDD)	Mali
Agencia de l'Habitatge de Catalunya	Spain
Agencia de Compras y Contrataciones Estatales	Uruguay
Agencia Nacional de Contratación Pública -Colombia Compra Eficiente-	Colombia
Agency for Public Management and eGovernment - Difi	Norway
AGRIDEV-CTT	Tunisia
AHU Enterprise	Pakistan
American National Standards Institute	USA
Arnika - Toxics and Waste Programme	Czech Republic
Bank of Zambia	Zambia
BIFMA	USA
Biodiversity International	Italy
Brasilia's Environmental Institute	Brazil
BSD Consulting	Switzerland
Bureau of Public Procurement, Presidency, Abuja	Nigeria
CAFRAD	Morocco
CATA (Farmworkers Support Committee)	USA
CEGESTI	Costa Rica
Center for Environmentally Sustainable Development	Bosnia and Herzegovina
Centrale commune d'achats	Switzerland
Centre de Recherche Scientifique de Conakry-Rogbanè (CERESCOR)	Guinea
Centre for Sustainability Environment and Planning	Ghana
Centro Mexicano para la Producción más Limpia	Mexico
Centro Nacional de Producción Más Limpia	Colombia
Chamber of Commerce, Industry and Agriculture	Lebanon
China Environmental United Certification Center	China
Cicloambiente	Chile
CIER	Tonga
City of Greater Geelong	Australia
City of Portland, Oregon	USA
City of Santa Monica, California	USA
CITYNET	Japan
Cleaner Production Centre of Serbia	Serbia
Cleaner Production of Lao PDR	Lao People's Democratic Republic
Cleaner Technology Centre	Malta
Collaborating Centre on Sustainable Consumption and Production	Germany

College of Environment and Safety Engineering, Qingdao University of Science and Technology	China
Commission Nationale des Marchés - CNM (National Commission for Procurement)	Madagascar
Competence Center for Sustainable Procurement	Germany
Concern Worldwide	Ireland
Consip S.p.A.	Italy
Construction Industry Development Board	Mauritius
Cornwall Council	UK
Corporacion Ambiental Empresarial	Colombia
COSEM	Tunisia
Court of Account	Lebanon
CP/RAC (Regional Activity Centre for Cleaner Production)	Spain
CREARTON	Mexico
CROA	USA
Croatian Cleaner Production Centre	Croatia
Crown Agents USA, Inc	Tanzania
CTBTO	Austria
CUTS International	India
DEFRA	UK
Departamento Nacional de Planeacion	Colombia
Department of Energy	USA
Department of Environment	Cyprus
Department of Health and Human Services	USA
Digital Government	Costa Rica
Diputació De Barcelona	Spain
Dirección de Compras y Contratación Pública	Chile
Dirección General de Administración de Bienes y Contratación Administrativa	Costa Rica
Dirección General de Contrataciones Públicas	Panama
Direction Marchés Publics/Ministère de L'economie et des Finances	Côte d'Ivoire
Division Regionale de l'environnement	Senegal
Dovetail Partners	USA
DuPont	USA
Ebony Center for Strategic Studies	South Sudan
ECLAC	Chile
Ecoinstitut	Spain
ecoLive	Switzerland
Ecosistemi srl	Italy
Egypt National Cleaner Production Center (ENCPC)	Egypt
Enda CACID	Senegal
Enterprise Promotion Centres Pte Ltd	Singapore
ENVIRO-PROTEC	Burundi
Environment and Development Foundation	China
Environmental Protection Authority	USA
EPEAT	USA
Equitable Origin	Ecuador
ESPAP	Portugal
Eurodad	Belgium

European Commission, JRC, IPTS	Spain
Federal Environment Agency	Germany
Federal Office for the Environment	Switzerland
Federal Public Planning Service for Sustainable Development	Belgium
FEKIH Salem	Tunisia
Florida Atlantic University	USA
FMYI [for my innovation]	USA
Forest Stewardship Council US	USA
Forest Stewardship Council International	Mexico
Fujitsu Limited	Japan
Fundação Getulio Vargas - Center of Studies in Sustainability	Brazil
Fundación Chile	Chile
General Services Administration	USA
General Statistics Office of Viet Nam	Viet Nam
Geneva Canton (Canton de Genève)	Switzerland
Ghana Revenue Authority	Ghana
GIZ (Deutsche Gesellschaft für internationale Entwicklung)	Germany
Global to Local Ltd	UK
Government of Flanders	Belgium
Government Procurement Policy Board - Technical Support Office	Philippines
Government Procurement Supervisory Authority	Peru
Green Council	China
Green Purchasing Network Malaysia	Malaysia
Green Seal, Inc.	USA
GSR Environmental Consultancy Sdn Bhd	Malaysia
Haut Commissariat à la Réforme de l'Etat, Présidence de la République	Guinea
Hewlett-Packard	Sweden
High Tender Board (HTB)	Yemen
Higher Education and Scientific Research in Tunisia	Tunisia
IEC	Switzerland
Independent Consultant	Mexico
Independent Consultant	Costa Rica
Independent Consultant	Mexico
Independent Consultant	Egypt
Independent Consultant	Croatia
Independent Consultant	Bahamas
Independent Consultant	USA
Indian Railways	India
Inèdit Innovació S.L.	Spain
Inside Matters	USA
Institut des Finances Basil Fuleihan	Lebanon
Institut Supérieur de Comptabilité et Administration des Entreprises (ISCAE)	Tunisia
Institute for Environmental Research and Education	USA
International Centre for Theoretical Physics, Trieste, Italy	Italy
International Criminal Tribunal for the former Yugoslavia	Netherlands
International Institute of Administrative Sciences	Belgium
IRAM	Argentina

Italian Cooperation	Italy
ITC	Switzerland
Japan Environment Association	Japan
Kayama - Center for Sustainable Design	Israel
King County	USA
Korea Environmental Industry and Technology Institute	Republic of Korea
Lawrence Berkeley National Laboratory	USA
Lebanese Cleaner Production Center	Lebanon
Leeds City Council	UK
Libyan Academy of Postgraduate Studies	Libya
Liseed Consulting	USA
Little Angels of the Environment Cameroon	Cameroon
Liz Muller and Partners	USA
LNEG-National Laboratory of Energy and Geology	Portugal
Malaysia Productivity Organization	Malaysia
Malaysian Green Business Association (MAGBA)	Malaysia
Middle East Technical University	Turkey
Ministère de l'Industrie et du Commerce	Benin
Ministère du commerce/direction de la promotion du commerce exterieur	Mauritania
Ministerio de agricultura, alimentación y medio ambiente	Spain
Ministerio de Ambiente y Desarrollo Sostenible	Colombia
Ministerio de Hacienda	Costa Rica
Ministerio de Medio Ambiente y Recursos Naturales	Dominican Republic
Ministério do Meio Ambiente	Brazil
Ministerio Obras Públicas y Transportes (MOPT)	Costa Rica
Ministry of Public Service	Uganda
Ministry for Ecology, Sustainable Development and Energy	France
Ministry of Ecology and Nature Protection	Senegal
Ministry of Environment	Lithuania
Ministry of Environment and Natural Resources (SEMARNAT-MEXICO)	Mexico
Ministry of Environment and Protection of Land and Sea	Italy
Ministry of Environment and Water	Bulgaria
Ministry of Finance	Slovenia
Ministry of Finance	Saint Lucia
Ministry of Finance	Kuwait
Ministry of Finance and Economic Development	Mauritius
Ministry of Finance	Malaysia
Ministry of Finance, Economic Affairs, Planning and Social Security	Saint Lucia
Ministry of Health and Social Welfare	Liberia
Ministry of Health and Quality of Life	Mauritius
Ministry of Labour and Social Welfare	Albania
Ministry of National Development	Hungary
Ministry of Planning and Investment	Viet Nam
Ministry of Production, Environment, Energy, Handcraft and Industry	Comoros
Ministry of Territory and Sustainability	Spain
Ministry of the Environment	Finland
Ministry of the Environment	Austria

Morogoro Municipal Council	Tanzania
Myrianthus Fosi Foundation for Biodiversity Conservation and Environmental Protection, B.P. 13669 Yaounde, CMR	Cameroon
National Association of Counties (NACo)	USA
National Centre for Sustainable Production and Consumption	Romania
National Cleaner Production Centre - Costa Rica	Costa Rica
National Environment Agency	Singapore
National Labour Commission	Ghana
National Procurement Ltd. Denmark	Denmark
National Public Procurement Agency	Indonesia
National Water Supply and Sanitation Project (financed by the World Bank in Azerbaijan)	Azerbaijan
Natural Resources Defense Council (NRDC)	USA
NCPC EL SALVADOR	El Salvador
NCPC-SA, CSIR	South Africa
NL Agency	Netherlands
Office Depot	USA
Oficina Normativa de Contratación y Adquisiciones del Estado (ONCAE)	Honduras
ONSSA	Morocco
Permanent Mission	USA
Plant Research International, Wageningen UR	Netherlands
Prime Ministry (The National Observatory of Public Procurements)	Tunisia
Procurement Policy Office	Mauritius
Procurement Watch Inc.	Philippines
Proyecto Wapí, energía	Nicaragua
Public and Private Development Centre	Nigeria
Public Procurement Agency	Bulgaria
Public Procurement Office	Poland
Quy Nhon City Environmental Sanitation Project Management Unit	Viet Nam
SAI	USA
Secrétariat Intérimaire du Volet Environnement du NEPAD - SINEPAD/Env	Senegal
SEMARNAT	Mexico
Service des achats de l'Etat	France
Slovak Environmental Agency	Slovakia
Sofres Liban	Lebanon
State Secretariat for Economic Affairs, SECO	Switzerland
Super Chemdry	Malaysia
Suranaree University of Technology	Thailand
Sustainability Dashboard Tools	USA
Susteco AB	Sweden
Swedish Environmental Protection Agency	Sweden
Tanzania Public Service College	Tanzania
TCO Development	Sweden
Televisión y Radio de Ecuador E.P. RTVECUADOR	Ecuador
Tenaga Nasional Berhad	Malaysia
The Catalan Office for Climate Change. Ministry of Territory and Sustainability	Spain
The Danish Environmental Protection Agency	Denmark

The National Observatory of Public Procurements	Tunisia
The Procurement Monitoring Bureau of the Republic of Latvia	Latvia
The Swedish Environmental Management Council, SEMCo	Sweden
The World Bank	USA
The Sustainability Consortium (TSC)	USA
UL Environment	USA
UNDP	Lebanon
UNDP	Belgium
UNDP	Ghana
UNDP / PCDC - Procurement Capacity Development Centre	USA
UNDP Project at the Ministry of Finance	Lebanon
UNIDO	Austria
United Nations	Kenya
Università degli Studi di Torino	Italy
Université Laval	Canada
University of Calgary	Canada
University of Exeter Business School	UK
University of Mauritius	Mauritius
University of San Diego	USA
University of Tunis, Faculty of Law and Political Sciences	Tunisia
UNOG	Switzerland
UNOPS	Denmark
UNSAM	Argentina
USDA National Organic Program	USA
Viet Nam Environment Administration	Viet Nam
Weyerhaeuser Inc	USA
World Fair Trade Organization	Netherlands